Bernard Percy, educator, writer, and creator of children's stories, books, and plays, is an active proponent of educational programs that offer a safer, saner, and more enriching growth environment for children.

Richard Royce is a well-known American artist. His works have recently appeared in eight museums, including The Smithsonian Institute Traveling Exhibition Service. He is one of the leaders in the field of cast-paper prints.

Bernard Percy

HELP YOUR CHILD IN SCHOOL

A SPECTRUM BOOK

PRENTICE-HALL, INC., *Englewood Cliffs, New Jersey 07632*

Library of Congress Cataloging in Publication Data

PERCY, BERNARD.
  Help your child in school.

  (A Spectrum Book)
  Bibliography: p.
  Includes index.
  1. Home and school. 2. Study, Method of.
  3. Education—United States. 4. Domestic
  education. I. Title.
  LC225.P47   371.3'02813   79–20009
  ISBN   0-13-386235-6
  ISBN   0-13-386227-5 pbk.

Editorial/production supervision
  and interior design by Heath Silberfeld
Illustrated by Richard Royce
Manufacturing buyer: Cathie Lenard

A SPECTRUM BOOK

Printed in the United States of America

10   9   8   7   6   5   4   3   2   1

PRENTICE-HALL INTERNATIONAL, INC., *London*
PRENTICE-HALL OF AUSTRALIA PTY. LIMITED, *Sydney*
PRENTICE-HALL OF CANADA, LTD., *Toronto*
PRENTICE-HALL OF INDIA PRIVATE LIMITED, *New Delhi*
PRENTICE-HALL OF JAPAN, INC., *Tokyo*
PRENTICE-HALL OF SOUTHEAST ASIA PTE. LTD., *Singapore*
WHITEHALL BOOKS LIMITED, *Wellington, New Zealand*

This book is dedicated to my daughter Charlene
and my godson Brian,
who are representative
of the children of the world . . .
may the very best
be the very worst you know.

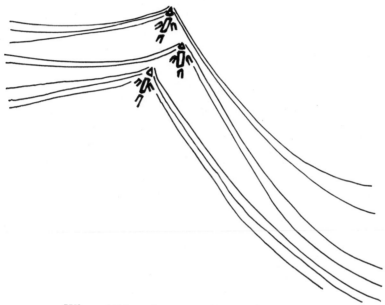

When children become unimportant to society,
that society has forfeited its future.
L. Ron Hubbard

Contents

chapter 3
Reading—A Basic Survival Tool 31

chapter 4
How to Study 56

chapter 8
The Importance of Good Nutrition 130

chapter 9
Health and Fitness 146

chapter 13
The Junior High School Years—A Time of Change   195

chapter 14
Some Final Thoughts   213

Preface

Every June, while teaching elementary school in New York City, I was given a list of the children who would be in my next year's class. I always looked down the list hoping to see the names of certain families whose children I knew would be responsible, spirited, pleasant, outgoing, and good students.

When I had the pleasure of teaching children from these families, I would meet the parents and seriously suggest they write a book explaining how to raise children, because they were obviously doing something right that should be shared with other parents.

I found that these parents did not "pass the buck" when it came to their children's schooling. They realized that for children to receive a successful education, parents must work and share the responsibilities with their children and the schools. These parents knew, or were willing to learn, what they could and should do to help their children get the most out of the school experience.

Parents are increasingly assuming more responsibility for their children's schooling. Parents really hold the key to how well children do in school; they *must* become informed and interested "watchdogs," guides, and motivators for their children and the schools.

The purpose of *Help Your Child in School* is to help answer parents' most frequently asked questions about their children's schooling: "What *can* I do?" and "What *should* I do?" With the answers to these questions, parents will be able to assume a more knowledgeable and responsible role in their children's education.

The book is a practical guide to help parents develop an understanding of what *the ideal educational situation* should be for their children, to observe what *the existing situation* is, and to know how to bring about the needed changes so the existing situation approaches, as closely as possible, the ideal.

Help Your Child in School covers topics of common concern to parents of children who are in school or soon to enter school. Every chapter (except the last) presents a basic viewpoint about a particular subject, with helpful and practical information and ideas to increase the reader's understanding of the topic, and a final section, "Things to Do," based on the data and understanding developed in the chapter.

You are encouraged to read the book with the intention of finding ideas and viewpoints that are real to you and that you agree with; use these to help your child best survive his schooling. Persist in becoming a more interested, knowledgeable, and aware parent—one who refuses to "pass the buck." The future of your child is at stake; it is in your hands. Enjoy the challenge of helping to educate your child; he or she will become happier, smarter, and better educated, and you'll have the satisfaction of knowing you helped!

As an added note, though the book is written for parents, it can certainly be read and used by anyone interested in improving the quality and success of his or her own, or someone else's, schooling.

If you would like to communicate with me as a result of reading this book, please do so by writing to me at 1250 S. Arlington Avenue, Los Angeles, CA 90019. I would enjoy hearing from you and will be happy to respond to any thoughts, questions, or feelings you'd care to share.

Thank you is a wonderful way to tell people who have been helpful that they are appreciated. There have been many people who have been helpful in the creation of this book.

Thank you—Vic Smith, Cam Smith Solari, Sheila Mackenzie, Greg Zerovnik, John Pisciotta, Nancy Hawkins, and Bill Schiff for sharing your thoughts and suggestions for this book; you really helped.

To Donna Sanford, Davina Rubin, Scotty Rigensberg, Adele Rossé, Dan DiVito, Dianne Philips, Virginia Fair, Renata Ganton, Sue Anderson, and Jeff Dubron—a special thanks for your extra time, effort, and contributions to the book; you were great.

To my wife Carolyn—you were there when I needed you—accept yet another acknowledgment from an appreciative husband.

A final thank you to L. Ron Hubbard—a man who really cares and whose knowledge was an invaluable source of help to me in the creation of the book. His data, viewpoints, and philosophy on education are the most workable and practical I've come across and are presented throughout the book, especially in the chapters How to Study and How to Develop Good Work Habits (the chapters I consider the most important to understand, use, and ensure that your child successfully survives his/her school experience).

chapter 1

How to Develop Good Work Habits

BASIC VIEWPOINT

Good work habits are abilities the student needs to easily start, continue, and successfully complete (that is, accomplish the purpose of) any task, assignment, or activity, so there is no longer any need to give it attention.*

It's important that your child gets control over her** work habits—without this control, feelings of anxiety, frustration, failure, and incompetence will develop.

The thoughts and efforts children (and adults) use to keep from starting and/or completing something successfully could easily be the topic for the thickest book ever written.

---

* The material for this chapter is based on the data and viewpoints developed by L. Ron Hubbard, educator and philosopher, as expressed in his writings, including the books: *The Problems of Work* and *Child Dianetics*. I've also used two books based on his writing as a source of information: *Miracles for Breakfast* by Ruth Minshull and *Fundamentals of Success* by Peter Gillham (see Bibliography for a more complete listing of books). All material taken from the copyrighted work of L. Ron Hubbard is additionally copyrighted © 1979 by L. Ron Hubbard. All Rights Reserved.

** I have chosen to alternate between the masculine and feminine pronouns by chapter, except when discussing a specific individual.

"I'm too tired."

"It's much too hard to complete."

"It's not really important anyway."

"I must eat something first, so I'll have the energy to do the work."

"I'll have to finish later—I've got to rest up for *next year's* volleyball game."

"I know this is the *348th pencil I've sharpened*, but I haven't gotten the point exactly the way I want it."

These and countless other even more creative thoughts and efforts help to increase the number of never started and/ or incomplete tasks and assignments children have. Every failure to do what must be done acts as an increasing burden on children, stopping them more and more.

Difficulty with school, and in life, can be measured by the number of never started or incomplete activities, tasks, or assignments a child has. But you can help your child develop the willingness and ability to start, continue, and successfully complete her work.

As you read this chapter, remember that the sophistication and methods you use when you apply the data will vary depending on the age, needs, abilities, and awarenesses of the individual child.

NO "REAL" TROUBLE

In 1964, while studying for my master's degree at Columbia University Teacher's College, I decided to do substitute teaching in some inner-city elementary schools. I knew I was well-prepared. I had majored in education, was a terrific student teacher, had worked very successfully the two previous summers with inner-city children, loved kids (and knew they loved me), and was six feet and one inch of "athletic manliness."

Let me describe my first day of substituting by saying that at 2:55 P.M. I had no trouble lining up the children to go home—all *ten* of them. The other fifteen had run out of the room or disappeared earlier in the day.

My second day with a different class was a much greater success. I had no "real" trouble lining up the *fifteen* who remained in class to be dismissed.

I went home, put my head between my hands, and thought about becoming a plumber or a disc jockey or . . . you get the picture. Then I realized what I had failed to do. I had not established that I was their *teacher* for the day, not just a substitute. And I had not *created their interest and agreement,* so that they'd accept me as their teacher.

I worked out what I had to do to establish the above viewpoints and agreements with any class I substituted for. The change was fantastic! Children literally did not want to leave the room at three o'clock. Once, when I was passing a class in the hall that I'd worked with a week before, they started cheering me. Their teacher looked at me with amazement and asked, "What did you do to them?" I told her, "I established some basics."

The section that follows is about what basics you have to establish with your children so that they will be able to develop and improve their work habits.

THE BASICS FOR ESTABLISHING GOOD WORK HABITS

Let Your Child Contribute and Take Responsibility

It's most important that children be allowed to contribute to others, especially in return for the help they've received. Allowing your child to take responsibility and make some contribution will help her become more capable, happier, and confident about herself and what she can do. She will then be on her way to developing excellent work habits.

Children gradually become more responsible as they are given things to do. I know a family with children who are 16 months, 6 years, and 10 years old. Their parents see to it that each child has some area of responsibility. Charlene, the 16-month-old, puts food away in the refrigerator with the help of one of the older children, mom, or dad. She also takes things to the garbage when asked. The 6-year-old, Dhyana, helps to fold and put away the laundry. Ely, the 10-year-old, prepares breakfast for the family every Saturday morning (and not just cereal in a bowl; he takes orders from each family member the night before).

Remember, once a child has agreed to take responsibility for a job that she is capable of doing, that child must be allowed to complete the job. Let the child know that you expect the job to be done by her and no one else.

Also, it is important to let your child know you *believe* she can do the job. Avoid threats that indicate lack of trust. For example, don't say, "If you don't do the job, you'll have to go to bed early."

Be prepared for mistakes and clumsiness at times, and avoid interrupting and correcting as the work is being done. Let your child do things at her own comfortable pace, but be firm; once she agrees to do a job, *accept no excuses* for its not being done. Above all, be patient.

The more responsibility your child is able to assume, the more easily she'll develop good work habits. So be sure your child is given something she can do.

Help Your Child Keep Meaningfully Busy

There's a saying, "If you want something done, give it to a busy person." I'd like to suggest, "If you want something done, give it to a busy child." Children want to help, work, and contribute. They have a desire and a need for activity. Even toddlers love to put things away, bring things to you, and smile that smile they know makes you happy.

It's important to give your child the right amount to do. If she has too much, she won't be able to finish all the jobs or activities—she may do her work poorly just to get it out of the way so she can get on to the next job. If she has too little to do, she may lose enthusiasm and become bored and lazy. Children who have too little to do often tend to create problems just to have something to do. Arguments and fights between family members decrease when they are all too busy to fight. Children who are kept meaningfully busy, with the right amount to do, establish for themselves a pattern of behavior that will carry over into their schoolwork and help them to develop good work habits.

Help Your Child Become Aware of Her Potential for Improvement

When children lack the knowledge and certainty that they can become better and more capable, they tend to get frustrated easily and quit trying when they encounter obstacles. Show your approval and recognition whenever your child has become better and more capable and provide opportunities for this to happen.

Teach your toddler where to put her toys; help your 3-year-old make toast; show your 7-year-old how to do a simple magic trick; let your 12-year-old help you fix your car. The possibilities are limitless. You can show your approval and recognition *verbally*—"That's wonderful," "You really are getting better"—or *actively,* with a hug, a kiss, a handshake, or a reward such as a special trip. The self-satisfaction and pride your child feels when she knows she is getting better and more capable are feelings of special beauty and value. *There can be no substitute for belief in oneself.*

Find Out Your Child's Feelings and Thoughts

It is vital for you to make a special effort to find out what your child's feelings and viewpoints are when she is unwilling or unable to start, continue, or complete her work. To do this there are three things to remember:

1. *Listen attentively* to your child's feelings and considerations.
2. *Avoid any evaluating*—don't, for example, try to explain to her why she is feeling what she feels. Don't say, "You're upset because you really don't like having a man for a teacher."
3. *Avoid any invalidation.* Don't make her wrong for the way she feels and thinks. Don't say, "The fact that you don't want to do it proves how lazy you are!"

There are many reasons for a child's failure to start, continue, or complete something. For example:

1. There may be no interest.
2. Daydreaming may cause loss of concentration.
3. The child may be emotionally upset.
4. She may have had too many failures. (Failures tend to cause people to stop trying.)
5. She may be bored or discouraged.
6. She may not be getting real satisfaction or enjoyment from her work.
7. She may feel there is no meaningful purpose for what she's working on.
8. She may be in love.
9. She may be excited about an upcoming or prior event.

Whatever her feelings or considerations are, try to fully understand them. Let your child discuss her difficulties and problems until her attention is no longer fixed on them. Often, just communicating about what is on her mind to someone who is really listening will help her handle all types of situations. *Avoid* letting her dwell on former difficulties and problems. When she has finished communicating her feelings, don't discuss or argue about them with her. Now that you've listened to your child, what do you do next?

Direct Her Attention to the Future

Show your child what she can do to achieve her original goals and purposes. What's important are the future activities and actions she undertakes. Work out with your child the steps she can take to attain the desired and/or needed results.

Avoid Accenting the Negative

Don't put your child's attention on her mistakes and failures by constantly pointing them out to her. This tends to lead to further wrong and negative actions. If you say, "Don't touch the glass—you'll break it!"—it's like an open invitation for her to do just that.

Focus your child's attention on the positive activities and actions she can undertake. When a child's attention is on positive actions, she will tend to *do* them. It's a lot more positive and encouraging to say, "You can complete the homework—do your best," than to say, "If you don't do your homework you'll be in trouble!" The importance of putting your child's attention on her positive actions can't be overstressed.

Practice What You Preach

A former student of mine wrote, "Look into your child and you shall see your reflection."* If you want to develop certain behavior traits and abilities in your child, it's up to

---

* In Bernard Percy, ed., *How to Grow a Child . . . A Child's Advice to Parents* (Los Angeles: Price, Stern & Sloan Publishers, Inc., 1978), p.36.

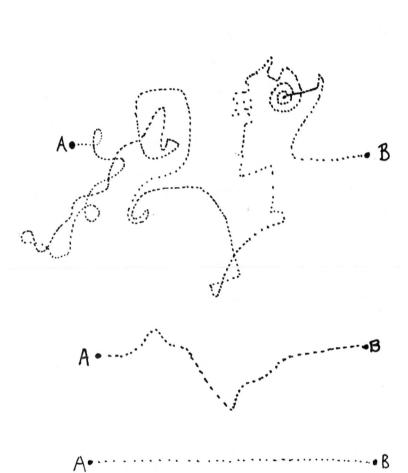

you to demonstrate the truth and workability of your intentions by what you *do*, not just by what you say.

On this, I need say no more!

WORK HABITS TO DEVELOP

The Decision Before Starting

To help insure that your child will successfully complete her work, it is vital that you help her *decide on what she will have when the work is finished.* By doing this, she will get the idea of having completed the assignment before beginning. It will be amazing how helpful this one simple thing will be.

So, before any task, assignment, or activity is started, have your child develop the habit of really thinking and deciding about what the end result will be. For example, before she begins doing her math homework, she should decide, "Questions 1 to 4 are correctly answered." In this way she will "see" a positive end result. Before cleaning up her room, your child should decide (get the thought), "The room is neat and straightened up!" Decisions such as "I'm going to . . . " or "I will . . . " are wrong ones to make, because they are decisions about *starting,* not about the end result.

Make a List of Things to Be Done

Have your child keep a list of things she has to do. As things are done, they should be crossed off the list; as new things have to be done they are added to the list.

Since not all tasks are as important as others, your child must decide the order in which they're to be completed.

Remember, before a child starts any item on the list, let her decide on the end result of the activity or assignment.

Things to Be Done	Things to Be Done

Date—Mon., July 5	Week—July 5–10
1. Math homework—p. 41, #3	1. Science report
2. Call Jerry about science report	2. Learn "Chopsticks" on piano
3. Practice piano	3.
4.	4.
5.	5.
6.	6.
7.	7.
8.	8.
9.	9.
10.	10.

Establish a Regular Time Schedule

A regular schedule that your child decides on and can follow will almost without exception improve her ability to successfully complete her work. She should schedule the time when work will be done each day, and within that time period, schedule how the time will be used. (See table, page 12.)

Help your child decide on how to use the two hours in the most efficient way, with the various assignments or activities for that day in mind. Help her schedule her study and work periods so they're not overlong; this will only tire her and make her restless and less alert. Allow for regular rest and relaxation times during the work schedule. It's better to have two to three short periods of study or work than one

Weekly Work Schedule

Time	Mon.	Tues.	Wed.	Thurs.	Fri.	Sat.	Sun.
A.M.	S	S	S	S	S		
9–12	C	C	C	C	C	Clean room	
	H	H	H	H	H		
P.M.	O	O	O	O	O		
12–3	O	O	O	O	O		
	L	L	L	L	L		Homework
3–6	Homework 4–6:00	Babysit 3:30–5:30	Homework 4–6:00	Homework 3:30–5:30 Cook dinner 5:30–6:50		Rake front yard 3–4:00	
6–9	Practice piano 7–7:45	Homework 6–8:00 Piano 8–8:45	Piano lesson 7:30–8:30	Piano 8–8:45	Piano 7–7:45		

long one. Also, help her balance "intellectual" desk-type activities with physical activities—for instance, one hour of desk work, then a half-hour art project.

Avoid Distractions X

It's important that your child keep her attention on one activity, task, or assignment at a time. When she is reading, she shouldn't also be watching TV, listening to rock music, eating a sandwich, playing a game of Scrabble.

It's so easy for a person to find things to do that will take attention from the work that has to be done. During your child's scheduled work time, help her develop the firm policy that any needless or unnecessary activities are to be avoided.

It is essential that your child work in the proper study environment—you will want to refer to Chapter Two for a discussion of the home study and learning environment (SLE).

Establish Policies for Work and Study X

Discuss and help your child establish work-study policies (rules, guidelines, and methods) on how and when she is to do her work. List the various policies and have your child sign an agreement to follow them. For example:

X 1. When I start a job I'll complete it! (I won't half-finish it and have to come back to it again and again and again and again and again ...)
2. I'll follow my work schedule.
3. I won't let other things distract me.

Signed: _____

Keep a Record Showing Work Accomplished

The record could be in the form of a chart, or a statistic sheet. Its purpose is to show your child how well she is doing. She should decide on what data should be recorded—for example, the number of completed tasks and assignments, the amount of time spent doing work each day, or the like.

If there is a change in the graph or chart, find out what caused it. If it's a good change, the child should continue whatever it was that made it good. If she accomplished less, she should find out what changed and correct it.

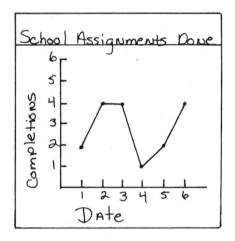

SOME GUIDELINES FOR IMPROVING

Get Your Child's Agreement

First and most importantly, you must have your child's agreement before trying to get her to change and improve her work habits. She will only be successful if she has a strong intention to improve.

Help your child understand the benefits of developing good work habits. You can list with her the benefits that will occur: for example, efficient work habits will give her more free time; she'll feel happier, for she will accomplish more. Have your child cite specific examples showing how her life will improve ("I'll have more time to play ball if my marks improve, and I'll be able to get into that college"). After she has agreed to change her work habits, you'll have to help her see that she is responsible for *keeping* her agreement.

Be Prepared for Some Difficulty

Some initial confusions, upsets, or disorder may develop as your child's work habits are being changed. It's much like organizing your desk area. At first there will be a "mess" of papers, unorganized and strewn about, but as you persist in your efforts, order and organization will come about.

This is something your child just has to go through. Persist with the agreed-upon changes and the results will be the improvements you and your child want—particularly if you make a special effort to focus her attention on the positive things she is accomplishing by her own changes.

Begin the Changes as Soon as Possible

Help your child see the advantage of not waiting until next week—do it *now!* This will mean that the old inefficient habits are going to have to be discarded. Help your child recognize poor work habits and discard them. As my friend Vic says, "If it doesn't work, why bother?"

Check Your Child's Progress

Periodically discuss with your child how things are going. Help her, as needed, work out steps to handle any problems, allowing her as much personal responsibility for improving her work habits as she can handle.

✗ The Concept of Have, Do, Be

The concept of have, do, be can be very useful in helping develop your child's work habits. First, discuss with your child what she would like to *have* when she finishes her work, for example, a funny story for her creative writing homework. Then discuss what she has to *do* to have that funny story, for example, turn off the TV, sit down, and write. Finally discuss what she must *be* to do what she wants to do, to have what she wants to have, for example, be a writer (not a TV watcher), while doing her writing to have a funny story.

THINGS TO DO

◆ *Complete the basic checklist for parents.* Then decide on (1) what things you should *continue* doing, (2) what things you should *start* doing, and (3) what things you should *stop* doing. Make these decisions based on the final results you want to have with your child. It might be helpful to write up your personal policy for helping your child develop good work habits.

◆ *Reread the chapter and decide what things are most appropriate for your child.* List ideas as they come to you. Work out specific actions that will bring about desired changes and improvements. Discuss with your child what is to be done, get her agreement, and then help her follow through. For example: your child is always *meaning to* clean up her room, finish that model submarine, start taking piano lessons, and so forth. There are two basic approaches to helping her.

X 1. *Break down each thing to be done into small steps and have your child complete each step.* In cleaning up her room, have her first put one pair of shoes in the closet, then a little later all her clothes in one neat pile (not necessarily where they belong yet). A little later, have her fold all her sweaters and put them in the drawer. When she can handle it, give her a more difficult step to be done.

2. *Have practice drills in completing things.* Let your child do such things as sharpen a pencil, put books in size order on a shelf, wash the tires of your car, fold all the dinner napkins, put out the garbage. *Remember, before she does anything have her decide on the end result she'll have when she's finished.* After each successful completion, show your recognition and approval.

◆*Work to change and improve your child's work habits.* To do this, get your child's agreement; be prepared for some difficulties but be persistent; have your child begin using the improvements immediately; help her avoid continuing inefficient work habits; check her progress; show approval and recognition for your child's successes; and hold your child responsible for keeping agreements.

◆*Establish appropriate lists, charts, and graphs for your child and yourself.* Lists, charts, and graphs can be a helpful reminder and motivator. They provide a way of keeping and presenting important information. Decide on the type(s) of lists, charts, and graphs you and your child would like to develop. For example, have a blank piece of paper titled, "Successes for the Week." Both you and your child can list your successes for the week—generally, or for specific areas. You can each initial your successes.

Checklist for Parents

	yes	no	sometimes
Does your child make responsible contributions?			
Are you patient, but still insistent that your child complete a job by herself that she has agreed to and is able to do?			
Does your child have enough to do to keep meaningfully busy?			
Do you make a point of showing your approval and recognition when your child gets better and more able at something?			
Do you actively seek to provide opportunities and experiences for your child to: (a) make a responsible contribution?			
(b) keep meaningfully busy with enough to do?			
(c) become better and more able at something?			
Do you avoid the following while listening to your child's problems and difficulties: (a) - *Evaluation* (telling your child what to think, or what she is thinking)?			
(b) - *Invalidation* (making your child wrong)?			
Do you avoid putting your child's attention on *past* problems, difficulties, and *bad* habits?			
Do you focus your child's attention on: (a) future actions and activities?			
(b) her positive actions and activities?			
Do you practice what you preach?			

your successes for the week—generally, or for specific areas. You can each initial your successes. Add to the list as you and your child feel you have a success worth sharing. You can make up a *"For Me to Remember"* chart. Write down those points from the chapter and other sources of data and viewpoints you feel are basic to helping your child improve her work habits.

For Me to Remember

Put attention on rightness.
Avoid invalidating what she feels and believes.
Allow her to make meaningful contributions.

chapter 2

The Home Study and Learning Environment

BASIC VIEWPOINT

✗ You should work to change anything in the study and learning environment that lessens the ability of your child to concentrate and put his attention on whatever is being studied, created, or worked on.

The importance of a proper study and learning environment (SLE) should not be underestimated. If a child can't study or work properly because of disturbances and distractions in his environment, then that child's education is certain to suffer.

There are several things to consider in setting up a good SLE, which we will discuss in this chapter. After reading the chapter, analyze your child's SLE and see how it can be improved.

THE METAL CURTAIN

While teaching in Brooklyn, New York, I worked in several different classrooms. Of all the rooms, 326 was my favorite—mainly because of the *metal curtain*.

The metal curtain was the two swinging doors that divided the third floor into two sections. On one side was the "battle zone," and on the other was "tranquility base" . . . and Room 326.

Several things contributed to making the other side the battle zone: among them were the girls' and boys' bathrooms, a favorite haunt for runners, talkers, and fooling arounders; four classrooms with teachers of varying abilities to control and manage a class (from good to "you've got to be kidding"). One teacher would have made a wonderful air-raid siren with her loud, high-pitched yell, so often heard in the battle zone. The fairly long hallway presented a challenging runway for budding track stars.

"Tranquility base" had no inviting bathrooms, a fairly short hallway, three classrooms, each of which had a teacher who worked well with children. There was Bob "Mr. Mellow" Maran, Carolyn "my wife to be" Bell, and myself; the other room was for a reading specialist who worked with small groups of children.

I'm sure the students' ability to study and learn was greatly enhanced by being in tranquility base. There were far fewer disturbances caused by yelling, disruptive children, slamming doors, and irate teachers. Doors could be left open during hot weather to provide better ventilation. In general, children here could easily keep their attention on their work and activities because there was a positive, comfortable atmosphere and a minimum of distractions.

POSTURE AND FURNITURE

Poor posture during study (or anytime) causes stresses on the body, which can bring about various aches, pains, decreased circulation, and fatigue and/or sleepiness. The more your child's attention is on bodily discomfort, the less he will be able to control his attention and concentrate on what's to be studied.

In the past, the Chinese had a method to help develop and maintain good seating posture. The teachers would take a string and attach one end to the ceiling and the other end to the students' queues (pigtails). If, while reading or writing, a child's head went too far forward, there would be a yank on the hair, reminding him to sit properly.

Here are some methods that are useful in developing and maintaining good posture:

1. The back and neck should be straight, with the head tilting only slightly downward in the direction of the material being studied or used. *Avoid* letting the head droop as if the neck were made of rubber.

2. Horizontal desk and table surfaces cause the student to bend forward too much. The work surface should be at a comfortable angle from the horizontal. This can be done by leaning a board on a 2- to 3-inch block, or book, and then putting the material to be used on the inclined board.

3. Select the proper chair for study. A chair should be used that will help achieve the best weight distribution. The weight should not be centered on a small area of the buttocks; an improper seating posture can cause weariness, aching, and numbness of the buttocks. The chair's back should be slightly tilted backward, with the seating surface comfortably angled from the horizontal; this will provide the best weight distribution. The seating surface should be padded to help maintain proper circulation. But, avoid using a soft, mushy chair as they have a tendency to cause sleepiness and poor posture.

4. No one should sit in a fixed position for more than an hour; it is good to move around and stretch the muscles.

5. Avoid unusual positions, such as that of the "Yoga contortionist" (body every which way), the "rubber-necked whooping crane" (neck extended from the body and chin pointed toward the chest), the "hunchback of Notre

Dame" (self-explanatory), the "bring me some grapes" position (lying down, feet up in a soft, mushy chair or bed).

PROPER LIGHTING

X

Proper lighting is one of the most important factors in maintaining a good SLE. Poor lighting can cause eyestrain, headaches, and fatigue, and often leads to those famous words, "Mommy, I don't feel like studying anymore."

Here are some guidelines for proper lighting:

1. It's the quality and placement of a light that is important, not the amount (as long as a minimum level is supplied). The lighting of the area around the work space should not be much brighter or darker than the light hitting the actual work space. Too much contrast is not good for vision.

2. Indirect lighting (light that is spread out to light an area) is best, as opposed to concentrated, direct lighting of a small space. If the main source of light is too distant, as it usually is when a ceiling light is used, an additional desk or table lamp should be used. These lamps are best used 1 to 2 feet away from the material being studied or worked with.

3. Avoid any light source that can be seen by the student as he is working—for example, low-hanging bulbs, unshaded desk or table lamps, and so forth. These will cause glare, which distracts the student and can strain his eyes. A light that comes from over the shoulder helps to eliminate the problem of glare.

4. Avoid direct sunlight on the work area; it causes glare and is bad for one's vision.

5. Be sure the light source is working properly. Any flickering, especially in a fluorescent bulb, can be distracting and irritating.

QUIET ENVIRONMENT

Distracting and disturbing noises make it harder to concentrate and put attention on work. Though it is true that some people can tolerate more noise than others, a relatively quiet environment is most helpful for everyone.

To establish a quiet environment, follow these guidelines:

1. Select a quiet part of the house or room—one away from inside and outside noises.
2. Utilize sound-absorbing material such as rugs, drapes, acoustical wall and ceiling tiles, cork for the walls, and so forth.
3. Dummy headphones (silencers), earplugs, and the like are helpful. (One student I knew used to first put cotton in his ears, followed by ear muffs, followed by a woolen hat pulled over his ears, topped off by a set of headphones. He created his quiet environment!)

4. To cover up disturbing noises, use a constant noisemaker such as a fan or air conditioner. Undisturbing "soft" music (*not* the ZEEM ZOOM PLUNK YANG YUP variety of Top 40) can be an effective method.
5. Plan for a quiet family period during the day, for study and other activities needing concentration and attention.

VISUAL DISTRACTIONS

Try to keep anything that may visually distract the student to a minimum. The more attention given to the surroundings, the less attention given to the material being studied. There are several things you can do to minimize distractions for your child (or yourself):

1. Build a blind to prevent visual distractions and to help the student concentrate better. Your child should decorate and style the blind to his own liking.
2. Don't have the study area near a window that faces a busy street.
3. Have your child sit facing a wall.
4. Don't plan the SLE where the TV can be seen or heard.
5. Do whatever your imagination can conceive of; for example, attach cardboard to each side of eyeglass frames so the student can only see what is right in front of him.

PROPER TEMPERATURE AND VENTILATION

We've all felt the sluggishness that comes from an overly warm environment and the discomfort of a cold one. To avoid losing mental and physical efficiency, the SLE should be properly ventilated, heated, or cooled. For the most comfort, here are some suggestions:

1. Keep the temperature between 65 and 85 degrees. This is the most comfortable range. Check with the individual for his preference.
2. An additional factor in comfort is humidity. A level between 30 and 70 percent is comfortable for most people.
3. Keep the top and bottom of the window open to allow for proper air circulation in the room.
4. Avoid having the work-study area too near a radiator, a window, or any area in which there may be an extreme of temperature.
5. Make sure your child's clothing is proper for the room temperature.

Clothing, incidentally, should be comfortable—not too tight, itchy, or in any way distracting to the student. Also, many people have their favorite outfits for working or studying—it helps to put them in a better mental and emotional mood. It might be helpful to let your child select a special study-work outfit.

NEAT, ORDERLY, AND ATTRACTIVE ENVIRONMENT

The less cluttered and more organized a work area is, the better one can study. Materials are easier to find for use; it's a more pleasant, less distracting environment to be in; a student becomes more efficient in a neat, orderly area. Attractiveness gives the SLE that added touch that makes it more appealing to the student.

Here are some suggestions for attaining a neat, orderly, and attractive SLE:

1. Have your child label and organize drawers and shelves in which material and tools for study can be kept.
2. Help your child develop methods and systems that will keep the area neat and orderly. For example, use an In–Out basket; clean up the area after each study task is done; don't wait for a great clutter to develop before cleaning up.
3. Allow the student to decorate the SLE to his own tastes. The more attractive the SLE is, the more he will enjoy working in it.
4. Making sure the SLE is kept neat, orderly, and attractive often involves battles between parent and child. It is best to get your child's agreement to do something, as opposed to enforcing standards. Your task is to make your child see that keeping his SLE neat, orderly, and attractive will be helpful to him.

A well-cared-for SLE will enable your child to complete his studies more quickly and efficiently, leaving greater time for other activities. To help a child understand this, you might try using a stopwatch to time the search for materials in a cluttered SLE. Do whatever you find is helpful in getting your child's agreement to properly maintain his SLE; the benefits will be worth it.

THINGS TO DO

◆ *Evaluate your child's home study and learning environment.* Reread the chapter and then analyze your child's current study environment. Use the format given below to help you decide on how to improve the SLE.

Good Points	Bad Points	How to Improve the SLE

The areas to evaluate are the furniture, lighting, auditory environment, visual environment, the climate (temperature and ventilation), and the attractiveness and orderliness of the SLE.

◆ *Let your child be involved in establishing a comfortable and appealing SLE.* Help him create his SLE using the concepts presented in this chapter. Let him take as much responsibility as he can; the more he contributes to creating his SLE, the better. For example, your 7-year-old may not know the best chair design to select for his SLE, but he can choose the color of the chair; your 14-year-old can design the entire SLE within the limits of money and available space you allow him.

◆ *Use your imagination and available resources to create the best and most practical SLE.* The basic guideline for creating your child's SLE is that it should be a comfortable and appealing space that will enable him to maintain the best possible attention and concentration on his work. What you do within those guidelines is for you and your child to decide.

A simple yet very helpful thing you and your child can construct is an inclined board to help improve his posture while he is working and studying. You'll need a ¾-inch-thick piece of plywood or particle board, 24 by 15 inches. Using wood screws, attach a piece of wood 6 by 18 inches and ¾-inch thick; raise the large board 5 inches off the desk top. Put large rubber bands on each end to keep papers from sliding off the board. You can put a small piece of wood at the bottom to keep books from sliding off as your child reads.

◆ *Schedule a special study time for your family.* If you live in cramped quarters, one way of creating a quiet study environment is to establish a certain time during the day when there will be no TV, radio, or any noisy activity that will create any disturbance. Work out a schedule that your family will agree to, and make sure everyone follows it.

SOME HELPFUL READING

THE GREAT PERPETUAL LEARNING MACHINE, by *Jim Blake* and *Barbara Ernst* (Boston, Toronto: Little, Brown and Co., 1976). There is a section in this book devoted to setting up and organizing a child's work space, including ideas and other sources of information.

NOMADIC FURNITURE, by *James Hennessey* and *Victor Papenek* (New York: Pantheon Books, 1973). This book presents designs for desks, work spaces; it's a good "how to" and "where to" book.

MAKING CHILDREN'S FURNITURE AND PLAY STRUCTURES, by *Bruce Palmer* (New York: Workman Publishing Co., 1974). Ideas and designs for making children's furniture from cardboard and other inexpensive materials are presented in this book.

chapter 3

Reading —A Basic Survival Tool

BASIC VIEWPOINT

The ability to read with understanding is vital in helping your child successfully survive her school experience.

Reading labs, *reading* kits, *reading* books, *reading* tests, *reading* this, *reading* that, *reading* here, *reading* there, *reading*, *reading* everywhere . . .

It would be fair to say that schools place more money, time, effort, energy, and attention on activities and materials that are designed to help improve children's reading ability, or in some way utilize a child's ability to read, than on any other undertaking.

There is, rightfully, a demand from all segments of society that schools help children develop a degree of literacy (ability to read and write) that will enable them to attain the information, awareness, understanding, entertainment, and inspiration that will help them achieve their true potential in life. This demand recognizes how important a tool reading is for success in school, and for personal growth and expansion in life.

Asking a child with a reading problem to progress through school is like asking someone to swim with an anchor attached to her body. The sense of frustration and failure a child feels when she has difficulty in reading can literally destroy the chances she has for being a successful student.

I hope you find КНЙГа ИНТерéсная.

Did you have trouble understanding that last sentence? Perhaps you had difficulty reading those two last words. What if every page of this book had several words you could not read? I'm sure you would soon give up on this book. It's just that type of frustration that must be avoided or handled in your child's schooling.

КНЙГа ИНТерéсная, two Russian words, is read as kĭ/nē/ga/ ĭn/tĕ/rĕs/na/ya; it means *the book is interesting*.

IT'S GREEK TO ME

The expression "It's Greek to me," often means "I don't understand." That expression became very real to me one summer several years ago.

I wanted to get a better personal understanding of the types of problems children met in learning how to read. To do this I decided to learn how to read Greek, a language I did not know at all. I decided to keep a journal of my experiences, and relate any difficulty I had in learning Greek to those of my students learning to read English. To make it more difficult, I did not want any help or tutoring.

I went to the library armed with a notebook, two pens, and a desire to learn how to read Greek. One week later I still had my notebook and two pens, but *no* desire to learn how to read Greek! I won't bother you with the details—just let me sum up by saying that I felt so much frustration at the difficulty I was having that I decided I'd rather do *anything* than learn Greek.

What I realized from that experience was the importance of having someone help guide and motivate my learning; correct my mistakes; provide experiences that would make the language more real; increase my interest in the language; and provide opportunities for me to use and read the language in real situations. These are the very things you as a parent could and should be doing for your child.

In this chapter I'll present some basic viewpoints and information about reading, with specific attention on things you can do to help your child.

WHAT IS READING? HOW IS IT TAUGHT?

Reading is essentially recognizing what a written word is (if needed, putting sounds to the letters that form the written word), knowing its meaning, and understanding what is meant by the phrase, sentence, paragraph, and entire reading selection.

There are basically two approaches for teaching reading to beginners.

One is *the look-say, or sight method,* in which children are taught to recognize whole words instantly, without having to analyze or relate sounds to the letters and parts of the word. The meaning of the word is also known.

Another method of teaching reading is through *phonics* (learning the sounds letters make, alone and in combination with other letters) and *other word-analysis skills* (for instance, learning rhyming families—*at* as in f*at*, th*at*, c*at*; learning common prefixes such as *pre*—as in *pre*view, *pre*pare).

Children are really learning to read a code—for example, the sounds of letters in the alphabet (*b* as in boot), sounds of letters in combination (*bl* as in *bl*ue, *ph* as in *ph*one), sounds of common suffixes (-*ly* as in close*ly*, -*ing* as in com*ing*). Children are taught how to combine the separate sounds and parts found in a word to gain an understandable whole word (o/pen/ly becomes *openly*).

Today, various word-analysis skills, especially phonics, are emphasized, with children also acquiring a basic list of words they can recognize on sight.

The results of a basic reading program should be a student who has the ability to easily read a text, know the meaning of most of the words encountered (and know how and where to define those not known), and understand the thoughts and concepts behind what is being read.

WHAT PARENTS CAN DO

As parents you are *not* expected to be experts in reading, able to devise elaborate, detailed reading programs to enable your child to learn how to read with real understanding. Yet you must assume responsibility for your child's success in learning how to read. You can help your child a great deal, and the importance of your encouragement, support, and guidance must never be taken for granted.

There are certain basic guidelines for you to consider in helping your child learn how to read. (These guidelines apply to all aspects of your child's education.)

Assume Your Child Can and Will Learn

You must start with the assumption that your child *will* learn to read. To assume anything else will be self-defeating for you and your child. One of the biggest failures of parents and educators is their *under*estimation of what a child is capable of doing and learning.

A wonderful example of how I underestimated the capability of one of my students happened several years ago. I was teaching a class composed of children having the greatest academic problems in the fourth grade. One student, Eric, was a very quiet child who never voluntarily contributed to or participated in group activities and discussions. All my efforts and those of the guidance counselor had been fruitless, and we came to believe that Eric's inability to confront or take part in group activities was something we had to accept.

Until one day!

The class was discussing favorite movies, and someone mentioned a film about karate. All of a sudden, and I mean all of a sudden, Eric for the first time since being in my class raised his hand, waved his hand, circled his hand, all in an effort to get my attention. I had never seen him so enthused and animated.

What happened next was amazing. I called on Eric, not really knowing what to expect. He proceeded to take over the class for the next 45 minutes (I am not exaggerating when I say 45 minutes). He had everybody spellbound, literally hanging on his every word and gesture. Eric talked about, demonstrated, and performed scenes from his favorite Bruce Lee martial arts films. He was so good that the principal, guidance counselor, several teachers, and students from other classes came to watch his performance. Each time I felt Eric had finished, he found another thing to talk about, with ever-increasing enthusiasm.

I had never seen anything like it. When he finished, only

because it was time to leave for home, the whole class applauded and cheered his performance.

Eric taught me an important lesson that day: never underestimate what a child can do, or learn, *given the right motivation and set of circumstances.*

Be Interested

Your active, genuine interest in what you do with your child is a key to her success. It is best to involve yourself in those learning activities and experiences in which you feel most comfortable and interested. Find some other source for activities and experiences you feel are important, but don't really want to involve yourself with.

There are few better ways to form a positive, constructive relationship with your child than by expressing a sincere interest in the things she's involved in. It shows you care, and provides important positive motivation for your child.

Make Learning Experiences Enjoyable

As much as possible, avoid forcing learning activities or experiences on your child (and yourself). Learning should be a joyful experience for both the parent and child, the teacher and student; anything less can have a negative effect on your child's attitude toward schooling.

Build on Your Child's Interests, Skills, and Talents

To best involve your child in constructive learning experiences, find things in which she is particularly interested, skilled, (or) talented. Use your resources and imagination to provide appropriate activities and materials. A good exercise is to list what you know your child's interests, skills, and talents are; then you can build on them.

Provide Opportunities in which Your Child Can Experience and Demonstrate Success

The greatest morale builder is successfully achieving something—especially something that can be demonstrated to others and that will earn their congratulations and acknowledgement.

HOW TO PREPARE YOUR CHILD FOR READING SUCCESS

There are many things you can do to help improve your child's chances and ability to read well. We will discuss some of the more important ones in this section.

Actively Develop and Enrich Your Child's Language and Vocabulary

Talk *to* your child! Talk *with* your child! Talk *in front of* your child! Talk, talk, talk!

Reading depends on recognition of the sounds of a word's written symbols and knowing the meaning of words. The greater the language development (the more words your child knows), the greater the likelihood that she'll know the meaning of the word she's reading; this makes reading that much easier and more real to her.

Talk to your child at every opportunity. Don't underestimate her ability to know and understand what you are talking about. Even very young children can develop a rich and varied vocabulary.

Donna Sanford, who helped write the chapter on nutrition for this book, has a daughter, Dawn, with the richest, most expanded vocabulary I've ever heard for a two-year-old. It's not unusual to hear Dawn say, with complete understanding, things like, "It's obvious you can't remember the event." Everytime I visit with Dawn my chin hits the floor in amazement at her language development.

What contributed to Dawn's ability to speak and understand language was the way in which Donna and her husband Sandy spoke to her. They never used baby talk, or talked down to Dawn. They would carefully explain things to Dawn using their normal vocabulary and manner of speaking. Donna and Sandy knew Dawn would learn to understand, and she did.

So talk, talk, talk, and don't underestimate the ability of your child to learn and understand!

Create and Provide Experiences that Will Enrich Your Child's Knowledge of Her World

The more your child can relate the words she's reading to her real life experiences, the easier reading will be. For example, if your child reads the word *rainbow* after just having seen a rainbow, the word will naturally have more meaning to her, making it easier to read and remember.

Experiences can be as varied and infinite as your own imagination, capability, and desire to create. For example, any trip you take—whether to a store, a relative's house, the country, Tibet, the library, a bank; any selective TV viewing; looking at a tree; opening your refrigerator—can provide wonderful opportunities for discussion, explanation, and learning.

Whatever you are doing with your child is going to be a learning experience. If you can build language and vocabulary learning into that experience, appropriate to your child's age, needs, and understanding, it will help your child learn to read.

Read to Your Child

A child learns a great deal when you read to her. The greater the exposure to books that involve and entertain your child, the more positively she will feel about books and reading. She can enrich her vocabulary, imagination, and awareness of the world with the experience she gains from your reading to her. She can observe how to turn pages and take care of books. The warmth and pleasure that you and your child will feel for each other as she sits in your lap or at your feet can only create a positive attitude toward books and reading—for both of you.

Read for Yourself

When your child sees that reading is important to you, that it's something you enjoy doing, the act of reading will tend to be more highly valued by her. A child learns by observing what *you* do, so it's important to model the type of behavior and attitude you wish your child to develop.

SHOULD YOU TEACH YOUR CHILD TO READ?

Yes, you should—and there are two basic requirements: you must want to teach reading out of genuine enthusiasm, not just out of obligation; and your child must be interested and eager to learn.* (If teaching is, or becomes, a chore and not a joy, however, it is best not to attempt it.)

If you are able to teach your child to read early in her life, you will increase her interest, involvement, and ability for reading and her overall achievement level in learning will tend to be higher.

If you decide to teach your child to read, you should remember several important things. First, be certain your child *wants* to learn; never force any reading or learning experience on her; the experience should be fun for her and you. Teach your child words she is familiar with and wants to know how to read. Avoid any communication—verbal or nonverbal—that shows displeasure with her progress and reading achievement. At all times, use the basics of study discussed in Chapter Four—"How to Study." Use your instincts and judgment about when and what to teach your child about reading. Finally, get as much information as you need to help you teach your child to read.

If you avoid any invalidation of your child's reading ability and attitude, keep the learning experiences light, fun, and interesting for both you and your child, and apply the study basics; you can then do no harm and can potentially do wonderfully well in teaching your child to read.

---

*Two books that can help you teach your young child to read are *How to Teach Your Baby to Read* by Glen J. Doman (New York: Random House, 1963) and *How to Help Your Preschooler Learn* ... *MORE* ... *FASTER* ... *& BETTER,* by David Melton (New York: David McKay Co., Inc., 1976).

As I write this section I've just come from visiting with Brian, my three-year-old godson. His mother is teaching him to read using the methods developed by Glenn Doman. Brian read for me two of the books his mother made for him, about his brother Eric and my daughter Charlene. He is learning beautifully.

My daughter Charlene, who is two-and-one-half-years-old, is also learning how to read. Every night she gathers up about ten books, takes them in bed with her, and goes to sleep surrounded by them.

You, too, can teach your child!

WHAT TO DO WHEN YOUR CHILD IS LEARNING TO READ IN SCHOOL

What if your child is in school? What can you do to help her learn to read? One of your key responsibilities is to *encourage your child to read*. Praise her efforts and successes; continue to expose your child to books and other reading materials that will interest her. Provide some books that are at her reading level, some that are easy reading, and some that will challenge her reading vocabulary and skill development. Let your child read to help you,—for example, ask her to look for a street sign while you're driving; have her read you cooking directions while you're at the stove; or ask her to ⌐ a letter that you're too "busy" to read. Allow your child ᶠrom a wide variety of materials that interest her— ⌐mic books, books on diverse subjects, school- ⌐-to" books, and so forth.

Writing is an activity that can be very important in helping your child learn to read. She can do *practical writing* (a shopping list, a letter to a friend, keeping her own diary). You can help your child do *creative writing* (a story, poetry, lyrics for a song). If she needs help in writing, let her dictate to you what she wants to write, and you can help her read it afterward. Writing can be a very useful aid for improving a child's reading ability; the interest factor is high, she will be familiar with what she is writing, and her motivation will be strong to read what she has dictated.

Ask your child's teacher what you can do. For example, find out what skills your child is working on that you could reinforce with reading activities at home. Ask if she has a

particular weakness in reading that you can help with, or strengths that you can help expand and build on. Get as much specific information as you can about what and how she is doing, and what and how you can best help her reading progress.

One of the most important things you can do for your child—in reading or in *anything*—is to help her find a *meaningful purpose* for whatever she is involved in. A strong purpose gives inspiration and direction.

Encourage or help your child find a meaningful purpose that she really wants to accomplish by reading. It is the greatest motivation, necessity, and requirement for a successful reading experience. Use your child's interests to help her find a purpose for reading something: if she has *an interest* in building model planes, *a purpose* for reading could be to read the directions for building a model plane; *an interest* in a particular movie star could lead to *a purpose* for reading a fan magazine article to learn more about the star; *a desire* to improve in some sport can lead to *an intention* to read a book on how to succeed at that sport.

EVALUATE YOUR CHILD'S SCHOOL READING PROGRAM

Because of the great influence of reading on your child's overall success in school, it is very important for you to evaluate the effectiveness of the school reading program. Find out if there is anything you can do to help change it, augment it, or support it.

How do you find out how effective the reading program

is in your child's school? You can discuss with both your child and her teacher the type of materials and activities that are being used—special reading kits and equipment, workbooks, readers. Ask about the general approach to the teaching of reading, for example, are the children grouped, or is it a completely individualized program? Find out how the program is making provisions for individual attention and guidance for your child.

Another thing you can do is to find out how your child is doing. Ask about her specific reading skills and needs. Look at, and have the teacher explain, any reading diagnostic or evaluative tests your child has taken to determine instructional level, skills, and needs.

Observe your child to see how well she is doing. Is she interested in reading? Is she able to recognize and figure out words? How well does she understand what she reads? How much voluntary reading does she do? Go over your child's work and spot-check her on it. Casually discuss her voluntary reading with her to see how well she understands what she is reading. Ask your child to read something to you that you need help with, for example, directions on a label while you're cooking.

Ask your child how she likes the reading program and how she feels she is doing. Get specifics from her, not just generalized statements—for example, if she says it's not any good, find out *why* she feels that way, and *what* is no good about it.

Get the teacher's evaluation of your child's progress, attitude, and effort in the reading program. Find out what you can do to help your child at home that will support the school's program. Discuss with the teacher, or any other appropriate person at school, any questions, or problems you find.

WHAT TO DO IF YOUR CHILD HAS READING PROBLEMS

If you find out by your own observation, the teacher's evaluation, your child's statements, or actual test results that your child is not reading as well as she should, find out *why*. To do this, there are some specific steps you can take.

Discuss the Situation with Your Child

Get her feelings and thoughts about what is happening with her reading. She may not think there is a problem learning to read, but is just bored with the school's reading program. She may have no real purpose for reading, or her eyes may hurt as she tries to read. Listen carefully to her comments and opinions so you will understand how she feels about the situation.

Discuss the Situation with Your Child's Teacher

Find out what the teacher considers the problem to be. Remember to put your attention on finding out *causes,* not *symptoms.* For example, statements like, "She never reads, so how can she improve?" or "She doesn't know how to sound out new words" are really statements of symptoms. What is needed are statements of causes: "She can't properly focus her eyes to read the print," or "She never understood what a vowel was and she is stuck at that point in her learning."

Ask the teacher what steps you can take to help your child. Together, you may be able to pinpoint the problems and solve them.

Check the Three Basics of Good Study

In determining the cause of the reading problem, be sure to check which of the three basic rules of good study, as given in Chapter Four, "How to Study," are not being followed and properly used.

The three basics are: be sure not to go past any misunderstood words; put as much demonstration, action, and realness into study as possible; avoid skipping or missing steps in learning.

Find Out What Changed

If your child was doing well and then began doing poorly, try to identify when she started to have a reading problem. Was her teacher changed? Was a new reading program started? When she lost her eyeglasses? Was it four months ago? Try to find what changed at that time that could have caused the problem. Handle anything that's found and return things as closely as possible to how they were when your child was doing well.

Finding the time when things changed for the worse and locating what caused the change have long been two of my most useful methods for handling the various problems of my students.

One particular example comes to mind, that of Yvette. She was a lovely fourth-grader, who had problems with her reading that she really worked hard to overcome. Yvette had a lovely smile that gleamed through her eyes whenever she did well in an activity, and especially after she had finished one of her written creations, which she felt very proud of.

At one point during the school year, Yvette's attitude changed and she began to just go through the motions of doing her reading lessons and stopped creating any written work. Her enthusiasm and involvement were gone. I tried several approaches to handle what was happening, including not saying anything in the hope that she would work through the problem herself. After a couple of weeks with no success, I met with her mother to discuss the situation. She too had noticed the difference in Yvette's attitude.

I asked Yvette's mother what had happened at the time Yvette's attitude had changed. The only thing she could think of was that Yvette had spent a weekend at her grandmother's house, just before we began to notice the change.

We called Yvette in and asked her if anything happened or had been said about her reading while she was at her grandmother's. Yvette started to cry. She explained that her grandmother had seen a story she was writing and noticed several mistakes in spelling and errors in the way she used some words. (These mistakes were unimportant to me on Yvette's first writing. We would edit her work together and correct these errors. What was important was her sense of enjoyment, accomplishment, and the specific reading skills taught based on her written work.)

Yvette told us that, "Grandma kept correcting everything I wrote, and when I asked her to please let me write the story by myself, she got mad and told me a girl my age should know how to read and write better, and that writing stories wasn't going to help me read."

With this information, Yvette's mother, who was very supportive and understanding about how important Yvette's writing was to her reading progress, discussed what occurred and was able to rekindle Yvette's belief and enthusiasm for reading and writing.

Locating the time of change for the worse, finding and handling the actual cause of the change, brought a great deal of satisfaction to Yvette, her mother, and myself.

As an added note, if there is a change for the *better* in your child's reading progress, you should locate the cause and continue what changed.

Have Your Child Take a Complete Physical Examination

It is possible that your child has a physical problem that is causing difficulties in reading. Special attention should be given to her vision and hearing. (See Chapter Nine, "Physical Health and Fitness.")

Check Your Child's Work Habits and Study Environment

See Chapter One, "How to Develop Good Work Habits," and Chapter Two, "The Home Study Learning Environment."

Be Supportive and Understanding of Your Child's Feelings

Not being able to read as well as expected and needed can be a very frustrating, demoralizing, and upsetting thing for a child. But you can help her in several ways.

Focus your child's attention on her positive qualities and strengths. Motivate her to read by providing material that she's interested in, and at her level of ability. These could be comic books, magazines, newspaper articles, advertisements, and so forth. Having your child write as often as she is willing, with your help as needed, is often a very effective method for motivating reading.

Maintain a positive viewpoint that will help your child believe the problem will be overcome. Validate any success, and where possible, have your child demonstrate her success to others.

If you find something that works to motivate your child to read, and/or helps handle her reading problem, continue to use it. It may be having a friend tutor her, or reading from everyday life materials (a phonebook, letters from family and friends, TV listings, labels from food containers, for example).

Maintain Awareness of Your Child's Reading Progress

From the beginning abilities of how to recognize words to advanced levels of comprehending and applying what is read, you must pay close attention to your child's progress. As soon as there are any signs of a reading problem, deal with them *immediately*. This isn't to suggest you should nag, pressure, worry, or upset your child by constantly checking, testing, and drilling her on her reading. But be aware and observant. Your child's reading ability is far too important a learning tool to be ineffectively taught and learned.

Dyslexia.   There is a learning disability known as dyslexia, which is an apparent cause of reading problems for some children. Dyslexia may cause children to write and see letters in mirror fashion (*d* for *b*, *q* for *p*), reversed, or even mixed up (*tar* for *rat*, *dfni* for *find*), and to have many problems writing and spelling.

To determine whether or not a child is dyslexic requires extensive testing, as many of the symptoms of dyslexia are often found in children first learning to read. The cause of this disability is not really known, but if your child has true dyslexia she may need special instruction and training.

THINGS TO DO

◆*Evaluate your role in your child's reading development.* Reread the chapter and use other relevant sources for information and viewpoints that you agree with and will help you evaluate your part in the development of your child's reading skills and interests. Find out what's happening with your child's reading progress by your own observation, through discussion with her teacher (if she attends school), and with your child. Then evaluate (1) what you are doing that you should continue doing; (2) what you are doing that you should *stop* doing; and (3) what you are not doing you should *start* doing.

◆*Survey your child's reading.* Here is a list of questions to ask yourself when you evaluate your child's reading ability and progress:

1. How much voluntary reading does your child do?
2. What material does she read? (Look at the subject matter, level of difficulty, type of material—books, magazines, comics.)
3. How much practical and necessary reading does she do?
4. How much reading does your child see *you* doing?
5. Do you and your child share reading experiences with each other? (Discuss what you read, read to each other, and so forth.)
6. How much assigned reading does she do?
7. When and where does she read?
8. How well does your child understand what she reads? (Make a point of discussing and questioning your child about what she reads. Be interested, not judgmental, in your approach.)
9. How does she apply and/or react to what she is reading?
10. Why is your child reading? (For information, inspiration, entertainment, or some kind of understanding?)

◆*Survey your efforts to teach your child to read.* Use the following list of questions as a guide. You can actually write out each answer or just use the questions to help think things through.

1. What is the purpose of your activity—that is, what effect(s) do you wish to create? For example, your purpose may be to interest your child in reading science books, especially books on airplanes, a topic that really interests her.

2. What do you know, or need to know, that will help you create the desired effect(s)? For example, *I know* my child likes airplanes. *I need to know* a museum or other resources where they have airplane displays.

3. What is your specific plan of action to create the desired effect(s)? (List or write out what you will do. Include how you will motivate and interest your child; present any specific data your child will need or want to know; actively involve her in the learning experience; conclude the activity, leaving your child with high morale and good feeling of satisfaction.)
   For example, I'll first take my child to the airport, then the museum to see and discuss airplanes. Next, she'll buy an airplane model of her choice (limiting her choice from among easy-to-construct models). She will then build her model (with my help as needed). The final activities will consist of going to the library to select books on experimenting with flight and doing the suggested activities at home.

4. What materials will be needed? For example, a simple model airplane kit.

5. How do you evaluate the activity? Include how you will know whether or not you created the desired effect(s). Review the activity for both successful and unsuccessful actions. For example: *evaluation*—my child is reading books on airplanes; my purpose was attained; *successful action*—allowing her to choose her own model for construction; *unsuccessful action*—going to the airport and museum in one day was too tiring.

◆*Schedule a time for reading.* Select a time during the day, perhaps just after dinner, for both you and your child to read privately or together.

SOME HELPFUL READING

APPROACHES TO BEGINNING READING, by *Robert C. Aukerman* (New York: John Wiley & Sons, 1971). This book discusses different approaches and reading programs to teach reading.

LEARNING TO READ—THE GREAT DEBATE, by *Jeanne Chall* (New York: McGraw-Hill Book Co., 1967). A comprehensive discussion of reading is presented in this informative book.

A NEW START FOR THE CHILD WITH READING PROBLEMS, by *Carl H. Delacato* (New York: David McKay Co., Inc., 1970). This book presents one viewpoint on the treatment (and prevention) of reading problems.

READING AND WRITING BEFORE SCHOOL, by *Felicita Hughes* (London: Jonathan Cape, Ltd., 1971). Ideas, insights, and practical advice abound in this book.

PARENTS, HELP YOUR CHILD TO READ! by *Ellen B. DeFranco* and *Evelyn M. Pickarts* (New York: Van Nostrand Rheinhold Co., 1972). This book has many ideas to use at home in helping teach your child to read.

READING, HOW TO, by *Herbert Kohl* (New York: E. P. Dutton Co., Inc., 1973). Information and viewpoints on how to teach reading are included in this book.

ᴀᴅ ᴀ Bᴏᴏᴋ, by *Mortimer J. Adler* and *Charles Van* New York: Simon & Schuster, 1972). This book __ actical data and helps expand a good reader's ability to understand and use what is read.

Tʜᴇ Gʀᴇᴀᴛ Pᴇʀᴘᴇᴛᴜᴀʟ Lᴇᴀʀɴɪɴɢ Mᴀᴄʜɪɴᴇ, by *Jim Blake* and *Barbara Ernst* (Boston and Toronto: Little, Brown and Co., 1976). The cover describes the book as "a stupendous collection of ideas, games, experiments, activities and recommendations for further exploration—with tons of illustrations."

Catalogs

Bookstores and publishers have catalogs available that can give you information about books that might be appropriate for you and/or your child. Some also list other materials that you can use. One of the best catalogs of books and materials on a wide range of topics such as creative arts, basic skills, physical education and movement, emotional and social growth, is published by:

The Children's Book and Music Center
5373 W. Pico Blvd.
Los Angeles, California 90019

Organizations

There are many organizations whose purpose is to help improve the learning and teaching of reading. Information should be available at your child's school, or from the reading (language arts) coordinator or specialist of the school district, about organizations that could offer information and assistance. One such organization is:

International Reading Association
800 Barksdale Road
P.O. Box 8139
Newark, Delaware 19711

This association offers eight small publications available at 50¢ each, including *How Can I Help My Child Get Ready to Read?*, by Norma Rogers; *How Can I Get My Teenager to Read?*, by Rosemary Winebrenner; and *How Does My Child's Vision Affect His Reading?*, by Donald W. Eberly.

chapter 4

How to Study

BASIC VIEWPOINT

Successful study is based on a child's knowing how to study and taking the responsibility to apply this knowledge to his education.*

Here are some often-heard statements of protest and dislike for school and study:

> "School stinks!"
> "Look, Ma—I have a 108-degree temperature—I *can't* go to school!" (After having placed the thermometer under the hot water faucet.)
> "I'm not interested in learning math."
> "That teacher is terrible! He doesn't know what he's talking about; I can't learn with him."

I'm sure you could add to this list from your personal experiences. Such protests have various causes, but the most basic one is that far too many children have never really been *taught* how to study and learn. Without this knowledge and

---

* I am indebted to Scottie Regensburg—teacher, educator, and parent—for her help in the research and writing involved in this chapter.

ability, children are bound to experience difficulty and possible failure in their education. Who would enjoy going to school, or studying, where only failure, difficulty, frustration, and upset await?

It's vital that parents be certain their children truly know how to study and then help them use this know-how in their education.

This chapter is about some basics of study that could very well change your child's (and your) life.

I've divided this most important chapter into two parts. The first covers the best, most workable method of study I've been able to find. The second part covers other helpful data and viewpoints that will help your child improve his study and learning ability.

JUDGMENT DAY

Judgment day for a New York City elementary school teacher is the day the citywide reading tests are given. How well your class does on the test is an important factor in how you're judged and thought of as a teacher.

In 1970 I was teaching the top academic fifth grade class. This was a wonderful group to work with, and the students were counted on to do well and help raise the average of all the reading scores in the grade (which they did). I was feeling great as I went over each child's test. The scores were averaging above seventh-grade level, which was "obvious testimony to my talents as a teacher," I gloated to myself.

I was planning the various modest ways of mentioning to the other teachers how well my class had done, until I came to Susan's paper. She has started the year reading a little above the fifth-grade level—an average reader. On this latest test she scored above the tenth-grade level. At first I really gloated: "Wow," I thought to myself, "she gained over five years of ability in her eight months *with me!*"

Then I remembered that Susan had been out of school for over four months. She had gone skiing with her family and missed much of the reading program I had developed for the class. Needless to say, my gloat disappeared very fast.

I began to think of various explanations—she got lucky; the earlier score was wrong; her four months with me were what had really helped; she'd probably had personal tutoring, and so on.

That afternoon I met her mother and told her how well Susan had done. I asked her what kind of reading program Susan had been studying while she'd been away.

"Susan just read books by herself," she answered. "She used to read a couple of books a week on her own and received no help from anyone."

While thinking of Susan's success with her own reading program, I somewhat amusedly realized one could draw the conclusion that my teaching had *kept* the other children from gaining an additional two-and-one-half to three years in their reading ability.

I began to question how much of an impact I made on the learning of my students, and how much of their gain was really independent of my input. I fully realized that the more personal responsibility children were able and willing to take in handling their own study and learning activities, the more success they would have in school.

The information on study that follows is vital for your child's success in school, and ultimately for his success in life.

If parents have a common dream for their children, it's that they grow and develop to their full potential in life. What a crime it is to let a child become miseducated, burdened with study problems that appear so complex even professional educators have difficulty handling them. What a tragedy to have these problems block their education, their potential life development, their personal goals.

The practical methods that follow can prevent or reverse the results of miseducation. Their simplicity will be experienced and enjoyed as your child is helped to truly learn *how to study*. The material for this section is based entirely on the copyrighted work of L. Ron Hubbard,* educator and philosopher, whose study technology is being used internationally on all levels, from preschools to universities. It is used with individuals of low, average, and high IQ.

A major source for this chapter was the book, *Basic Study Manual*, compiled from the works of L. Ron Hubbard by Applied Scholastics Inc., and which contains essays on study taken from his lectures, articles, books, and research notes; particularly *The Student Hat, Problems of Work*, and *Axioms and Logics*. (See Bibliography for more information on this material).

THE THREE BASICS OF STUDY

Put as Much Demonstration, Action, Reality into Study as Possible

A child can sometimes understand the words and theory of a subject, but still have an unclear idea of how something he is studying can be applied to his life. To handle this type of situation, balance the theory and thinking side of education

---

* All material taken from the copyrighted work of L. Ron Hubbard is additionally copyrighted © 1979 by L. Ron Hubbard. All Rights Reserved.

with demonstration, action, and the real things that are being studied.

There are several ways of doing this:

1. As much as possible, give your child the real things he's studying about. For example, if he is learning about fish, give him fish; if he is learning about adding money, give him money to add, and so forth.

2. Use household articles like buttons, blocks, dolls, and paper clips, to have your child demonstrate the meaning of what is being studied. For example, to help a child understand the meaning of the word *anger,* he can have a block symbolize one man and a paper weight another. Then have him move each piece in a way to demonstrate anger by pretending that one piece is yelling at the other piece.

3. Clay is a wonderful action tool. Allow your child to make a clay model of what he's studying. (This is, taking the *abstract* and making it *concrete,* helping your child to *see* and *feel* what he is studying.) The larger he makes the models, the better.

4. Your child can draw pictures, make a scrapbook, or even just look at pictures of what he is studying—this will help make an academic subject real to him.

5. When appropriate, role playing can be a good learning tool.

Whatever you can use to make the material studied more real and understandable for your child will be most helpful. Bored and apathetic children will become alert and interested. Teachers tell about children in their class no longer wanting to go to the bathroom, nurse, or other places out of the room, when theory is being balanced with demonstration, action, and reality. Certain symptoms, such as headaches, stomach aches, dizziness, or hurting eyes that may result from a child not having a proper balance of theory (thinking) with action, reality, and demonstration, can be handled.

A beautiful example of this happened as I was working on subtraction with one of my fourth-grade students, Kim. She was a very bright, articulate, outgoing child who had *never* learned to subtract properly. I was working with her privately in a room along with Crystal, who was preparing a chart for me which included a description of how certain physical symptoms can be related to a lack of action, reality, and demonstration in study.

I was handling Kim's subtraction problem by trying to locate any misunderstood word(s), when she began to complain about her eyes hurting and started rubbing them. I persisted, hoping to find misunderstood words, when Crystal whispered, "Pssssst," and waved a finger, motioning me to her. She then pointed her finger to the place on the chart where it stated, "*Hurting eyes*—lack of action, reality, or demonstration."

I kissed Crystal, went to Kim, and had her draw, use various articles, and look at pictures to demonstrate the basic subtraction concept she had been unable to understand and apply. After ten minutes of this, she was finally able to understand and use the concept 100 percent successfully in her subtraction work.

Kim, Crystal, and I left that room with a love for learning.

You can help your child use action, reality, and demonstration while he is studying; by putting life into a subject, the reality and understanding for that subject can only increase.

Avoid Skipping or Missing Steps in Learning

Unless a child is working at the right level, problems in study will develop. Skipped or missing steps in learning any new material is the second major study problem to know how to handle.

Skipped steps are most easily observed in learning a new skill or activity. The child is doing fine trying to learn something new and then comes to a step (let's call it step *C*) where he feels confused and uncertain. The apparent way to handle the problem is to try to get the child to understand that step he's confused on and having trouble with. The actual way to handle this is to realize that his confusion on step *C* is caused by something he didn't fully get on step *B* (or even possibly step *A*).

The child should restudy or practice step *B* even though he *seemed* to know or do it well. Have the child thoroughly understand and/or perfect step *B* then go on to step *C*. Continue forward, doing each step thoroughly.

A perfect illustration of a successful use of this study method happened with Charlie, a fifth-grade student of mine. He had never been able to write the alphabet from *A* to *Z* without making numerous mistakes, and he naturally had many reading problems as well.

Charlie always became very confused *after* the letter Q and could not correctly write the alphabet. For example, he would write *Q R S T V U W Y X Z,* or *Q R T S V W U X Z Y.* For years, teachers had tried every approach imaginable to correct the situation—from constant drilling and copying the alphabet to drawing pictures. They kept putting Charlie's attention on the area of confusion, the letters after Q, but his basic problem turned out to be (as I expected) the letter Q itself. It was at this point that things went wrong. The missing step was a thorough understanding of Q—its use, functions, sound, rules.

Charlie had never really understood the letter Q. I had him demonstrate and draw pictures of the Q and helped him see how it was used.

At that point, after correctly learning what Q was all about, we went over the whole alphabet. Charlie read it, said it, copied it, looked at various pictures of the letters, and so forth. Then it was finally time for him to write it all from memory.

I could feel Charlie's fear and hesitancy. So many times in the past a teacher had tried to teach him the alphabet, only to meet failure. The embarrassment, sense of failure, and frustration had been with Charlie for years, and if he failed again it would be another blow to his self-image (to say the least).

As he started writing, he zipped through the letters up to Q. He paused for an instant before going on. Then I watched the letters appear on the paper in the correct order— R S T U V W. I could see and feel Charlie's sense of relief and satisfaction. When the letters X Y Z followed, the look of joy and pride on his face was priceless. He had finally succeeded in learning the alphabet—all of it. That moment was very precious to both of us.

As an added note, it took 35 minutes from the time I started working with Charlie until he could finally write the alphabet correctly with ease—thirty-five minutes, using the correct method, to handle years of failure and frustration.

A child who misses or skips a step in learning can feel tremendous confusion; he might even feel the environment become unstable and start to reel around. Find the missing or skipped step and have the child do that step until he thoroughly understands and/or can do it. Then have him continue forward.

Be ready for many precious moments as you see your child attain the success and achievement that his confusion had kept from him.

Handle Misunderstood Words Immediately

During my first year of teaching, one of my students asked, "Mr. Percy, will ya lend me a dime? I got a *Jones* for some ice cream."

"You've got a *What?*" I asked.

"A *Jones* for some ice cream, Mr. Percy. You never had a *Jones?*"

"What is a *Jones* for ice cream?"

I had absolutely no understanding of what he was talking about. With a disbelieving look on his face he said to me, "You don't know what a *Jones* is? You sure don't know much, do you, Mr. Percy?"

I smiled and told him, "When it comes to *Joneses*, I guess you're right, but what is a *Jones?*"

"Let me say it this way—I just got to have me some ice cream!"

My education continued. A *Jones* is a strong desire or craving for something.

This story illustrates the most important thing for your child to know about study; lack of understanding a word(s) leads to a failure to understand what is being discussed or studied . . . which leads to difficulty in that subject . . . which inevitably leads to the student's dislike of the subject . . . which leads to . . . and on and on. I'm sure you can see where the trail ends.

It is *not* an oversimplification to say that a word(s) that is totally or partially misunderstood is the *greatest single cause of children's failure in school.*

When I first came across this information it sounded right, but I still wasn't convinced that a misunderstood word could be so important a cause of children's failure in school. I decided to observe the truth of this concept when working with my students.

I soon found that whenever a child got an answer wrong on a reading comprehension question, about 80 percent of the time it was *directly* linked to a misunderstood word or words in the material read or the question asked.

In math, I was amazed at how many children did not understand the basic *words* of the subject and how directly this related to their difficulties in math. Let me ask you—what's the difference between arithmetic and mathematics? Do you know? *Arithmetic* is understanding and using numbers in addition, subtraction, multiplication, and division. *Mathematics* is the whole study of numbers, measurement, and space. How certain you are about these two basic words helps determine how strong a foundation you have built to understand and use the facts and concepts of the subject.

To further help you understand the truth of this point, here are some things for you to think about:

1. Think about something you do well. Then look at the vocabulary for that subject or activity. I'm sure you'll find you understand the words you commonly use or come across.
2. Think about something you do poorly. How many words commonly used for that subject or activity *don't* you know and understand?
3. Ask your child to define and explain words in something he does well and in something he does poorly. Note the difference in how well the words are known in the thing he does well, as compared to what he does poorly.

Don't go past misunderstood words—and that includes "common" words as well as new or unusual words.

When he is studying, your child's major tool should be a dictionary that he knows how to use properly. Words your child is uncertain of should be looked up until their meanings are known. At that point he should use the words in his own sentences until he feels comfortable using them.

There are some symptoms that indicate that your child has passed over a misunderstood word. He:

Can't seem to concentrate on study
Can't seem to keep his place in the book being studied

Generally detests the subject

Wants to or actually does leave the study (even school) entirely

Feels blank about the entire subject (or part of it) being studied

Starts to get tired

May become disruptive or commit harmful actions in the area in which he fails to understand some of the words

May become lazy in his attitude and work

These symptoms can be handled in the following ways. *First,* find the last point at which the student was doing well in his study. Toward the end of that section, have the child look for a misunderstood word (remember, it can be a commonly used word as well as a new or unusual one).

Second, fully handle the misunderstood word by having the child look it up in a dictionary, understand its meaning, then use it in sentences until it can be easily and correctly used.

Third, have the student start at the point where the misunderstood word was found, and read forward, being careful not to pass over any *more* misunderstood words.

Fourth, if that doesn't take care of the symptom you wanted handled, go back even earlier in the material until you find the misunderstood word(s) and straighten it out with the above method.

It's possible that the first page of the book needs to be learned. In a very tough study situation (one that doesn't resolve easily) you could take all the important words relating to the subject and handle them by the method explained for handling misunderstood words.

The simple truth is that dictionaries and their proper use in handling misunderstood words can literally save your child's education and help him develop his greatest potentiality.

HOW TO HANDLE A SUBJECT
IN WHICH YOUR CHILD IS DOING POORLY

What follows is information on what you can do to help your child when he has trouble with a subject. This information utilizes the three major study methods just discussed. First you should discuss the trouble with your child. Try to find out at what point in the studies the problem began. How does he feel while he is studying (blank, tired, confused, bored, and so forth)? What does *he* think the trouble might be?

Determine which of the three major study points need to be used to handle the problem.

Sometimes there can be a variety of things causing a study problem. There could be misunderstood words; too little action, reality, or demonstration; steps missed, or introduced too quickly. It is important to remember that misunderstood words are the most destructive element and need to be sorted out first.

Here's a general example of what you might do to deal with your child's study problem:

1. Establish a *purpose* for studying the subject—make sure your child is in agreement with this purpose. (See pp. 69–74 in the next section—"Key Points about Study.")

2. Pick out some *important words* in the subject. Using a dictionary, help your child define each word until he no longer has to go back to the dictionary for its meaning; then have him use each problem word in sentences until he really understands how to use the word. If there is a problem learning a word, help your child understand it by demonstrating the word in a realistic way, using demonstration, action, or in some way relating the word to the real world.

3. When the words are understood you can *pick out some important rules* pertaining to the subject (if he is studying

gravity, he had better understand Newton's theories on gravity). Have him illustrate his comprehension of these rules or principles by doing something concrete, such as making a clay model, drawing, or in some way showing a total understanding of the important rules.

4. Once this step is accomplished, have your child *restudy the material* he didn't understand before, using all three study basics. If he had misunderstood words, he certainly won't retain any of the material unless he studies it again.

5. Keep working in this manner with your child until he is obviously able to apply what he is learning. Periodically, even after he is doing well, *spot-check* him for possible misunderstood words. If you find any, make sure they're learned right away. Watch how he is doing. If he's doing well, he'll be happy, willing to discuss the subject, and a pleasure to have around.

KEY POINTS ABOUT STUDY

Determine the Purpose of Studying

Find out what your child's purpose is for studying a particular subject. Before real understanding can occur, your child must have an agreed-upon purpose for studying the subject.

Ask your child what he hopes to have after he finishes studying the subject.

If your child does *not* have a purpose, discuss the ways the subject can help in his life; this is often enough to give him a strong reason for learning it.

Indicate to your child some things he will have from his studies that he may not be aware of—for example, studying English grammar will increase his ability to learn a foreign language, understanding geometry can help your child gain a better understanding of carpentry work he is interested in doing. The key point is to have your child determine for himself the benefits he'll have from studying the subject. A strong purpose for studying a particular subject automatically creates an interest in that subject, which in turn leads to your child's active involvement and increased responsibility for what's being learned.

Help your child clarify his purpose, and if indeed there is no real purpose your child has for studying, he *shouldn't* have to study.

Use Dictionaries and Other References

Your child *must* have a dictionary that is appropriate for his level of understanding. A good dictionary properly used is the most valuable reference tool he will have. Find a dictionary that will not frustrate your child with words well beyond his reading level, yet not so simple as to give incomplete definitions.

Your child should also have access to other reference books such as encyclopedias, almanacs, and atlases. He should know how to use these sources to answer his questions. Doing so will help him develop more independence in learning and studying.

Develop Understanding and Application

It is vital that your child understands and can apply what he is learning to life. Grades are an indicator of understanding, and have an importance, but don't let a high grade fool you into thinking that your child has truly mastered a subject.

The real test is whether or not he can apply what he has learned to life.

Find out what your child is learning by communicating with him and his teacher. Look at his notebooks, homework, textbook assignments, special projects. Then check on how your child is progressing by finding meaningful situations in which he can apply his knowledge. For example, if he is studying subtraction, have him pay the clerk at the store and check to see that he gets the correct change. If he is studying measurement, let him measure your table for a new tablecloth. For reading, have him read labels, street signs when looking for a particular street, a letter from a relative or friend; for art, let him decorate or redecorate his own room or make a birthday card for someone.

Encourage Self-Responsibility

You should always be concerned with what you can do to help your child develop personal responsibility for his learning. (See the checklist of the things you can do to help your child develop in this area at the end of the chapter.)

Don't see yourself in the role of one who only imparts information, but rather as a guide to help your child become responsible for his own education.

Let Your Child Say, "I Don't Know"

As a teacher, one of the hardest things to overcome was my students' reluctance to freely admit when they didn't know or understand something, and then ask the appropriate question(s). Vic Smith, educator and writer, wrote, "Make it ok for your child to say, 'I don't know.' "

Here are several things you can do to help your child feel it's ok to say, "I don't know":

Ask your child about things *you* don't know, that he will be able to help you with.

Show your approval whenever your child admits he doesn't know something he wants to learn more about.

Listen, don't berate or lecture your child when he has difficulty learning something.

If your child answers incorrectly, avoid being critical. Acknowledge his answer and decide which of the following things to do: Refer him to a good source for the information needed. (For example, when he gives an incorrect definition for a word, refer him to the dictionary.) Help him discover the correct answer—for example, have him check over his math work for careless mistakes. Tell him the correct answer (especially if *a* and *b* are impractical to do, making sure he understands why the answer is correct.)

To sum up, don't make a child feel ashamed or embarrassed when he doesn't know or gives a wrong answer.

Allow Your Child to Demonstrate His Skills, Successes, Gains, Knowledge, and Creations; Acknowledge and Validate Them

I used to run a sports club where I taught children to do flips in the air (I could teach it, but never had the courage to try it myself). Dennis was a chubby, not-too-athletic boy who more than anything wanted to learn how to flip. I spent a lot of time, sweat, and anxious moments watching him attempt his circular flight through the air. Many times I was thankful for his well-padded posterior (and so was he!).

When he finally learned how to flip, I stopped everyone's activity in the club and told them to watch Dennis. They were all aware of how hard he'd been working on the "no-hands" flip, and when they saw him do it successfully, all the kids in the club genuinely cheered and congratulated him. The validation and acknowledgement Dennis received from the kids added infinitely to the personal satisfaction he felt in being able to do the flip.

Let Your Child Know What He Is Expected to Do and Accomplish

Very often parents (and teachers) assume that because they gave a direction or instruction and the child is conscious, what was said was both heard and understood by the child. *Be warned.* Don't make that assumption. I can't tell you the number of times I assumed students understood the assignment, when they really didn't. It was really my flunk for not being certain my instructions were correctly understood.

Be certain your child is absolutely certain of what he is to do. One way to make sure you've been understood is to have the child restate, demonstrate, and/or explain the assignment or activity.

Help Your Child Develop Good Work Habits

See Chapter One—"How to Develop Good Work Habits."

Maintain a Proper Study and Learning Environment

See Chapter Three—"The Home Study and Learning Environment."

READING TO LEARN

A basic skill needed to succeed in the study of a subject is the ability to read. I am not referring to basic word recognition and comprehension skills, but the skill to learn data from a text.

What follows are a number of guidelines that will be helpful in ensuring that your child will be able to understand and use the material he reads.

Use the Three Basic Study Methods

Review the section in this chapter on the three basics of study. They are relevant to your child's ability to learn by reading.

Read with a Purpose

Have your child decide what he hopes to have after completing the page, chapter, or book—memorization of factual data? a general viewpoint about the subject? the ability to use the data? He should decide to attain that purpose before starting to read and study.

Be an Involved Reader

Teach your child the important points of being an involved reader. Here are some things you can help him know about constructive reading.

Survey the material to be read before reading. Skim through the pages, looking at titles, chapter headings, illustrations, topic sentences, to get an understanding of what is important (the main ideas, important details to be learned) as it relates to the purpose of the reading.

Question and think with the author. Do you agree or disagree? Is that fact important? Is the author answering any questions you have about the topic? How does the information relate to earlier information learned? *Think!* Don't just allow the words to hit your eye and fall back to the page.

Check and review for understanding. At regular intervals, your child should check to see if he remembers and understands what he has read by summarizing, paraphrasing, and demonstrating the material covered. Stress this data—don't read a whole book or assignment and realize at the end that he doesn't remember or can't understand and apply what he has been reading (studying). The more your child reviews and studies something, the more likely he is to remember it and gain increasing certainty about his knowledge and ability to apply the material learned.

In addition, by reviewing and checking his understanding and/or ability to apply the material studied, your child can quickly spot when he's running into trouble and can immediately use the basic study methods to handle any difficulty.

Your child should learn to read, so he can read to learn!

THINGS TO DO

◆*Review the chapter for specific problems.* List those points you feel relate to your child's study problems.

◆*Decide on what you have to do to help your child.* Make a list of specific things you will do to help your child—your program. Follow the steps indicated in the chapter to handle your child's problem. When you work with your child, remember to do the following:*

1. Work with the purpose of helping your child get a better understanding of the material to be studied.

---

* The first five points are from L. Ron Hubbard's *Basic Study Manual* (Los Angeles: Applied Scholastics, Inc., 1972). For information on this method, write Applied Scholastics, Inc., 955 South Western Ave., Los Angeles, Calif. 90006.

2. Intend that at the end of your working session, your child will be aware he is doing better and has more understanding of the subject.
3. Take up only one thing at a time and make sure your child does each step correctly before going on.
4. Give good directions.
5. Acknowledge your child and tell him when he is right in what he is doing.
6. Don't worry if you don't know the words or subject very well—you can always learn them later, but use the study principles discussed in the chapter.

◆*Be aware of how the three basics of study affect your learning and understanding.* Apply the information in the chapter to *yourself,* to understand it better.

◆*Educate your child on the information presented in this chapter.* You can have him read the chapter and apply the points presented in his studies. Help him see the workability of these study methods. You can help your child make up a chart listing major points to remember about study.

◆*To help your child become responsible for his own education and study, complete the following checklist.*

Checklist for Parents

	yes	no	sometimes
Does your child understand the purpose for studying a subject?			
Does your child know what he is expected to do and accomplish?			
Does your child know and use the three major study guides: (a) Not going past misunderstood words?			
(b) Staying in touch with the real things, demonstrating, or putting into action what is being studied?			

(c) Not skipping or missing steps on what is being learned?		
Does your child have and use the proper tools of learning (especially a dictionary, and things to make the subject more real and alive)?		
Can your child understand and apply what he is studying to life, and the things he is involved with?		
Can your child say "I don't know"?		
Does your child show and/or use the skills, abilities, or understanding he learns?		
Does your child use good work habits?		
Does he study in a proper learning environment?		
Does he know how to read to learn?		
Does he keep in peak physical condition?		

SOME HELPFUL READING

There are two books I highly recommend, both available from Applied Scholastics Inc. (See page 76 for address.) One is The *Basic Study Manual* and the other is *The Student's Study Course,* both compiled from the works of L. Ron Hubbard.

chapter 5

The Classroom Environment

BASIC VIEWPOINT

The environment of a classroom has an important influence on the tone, mood, and motivation of a student and can indicate how much meaningful education—learning, production, and creation—is taking place.

Entering an environment that is neat, orderly, and attractive—one that displays the children's learning efforts and imparts a positive feeling—is an enjoyable experience. There's a certain spirit in such an environment that immediately affects students, teachers, and visitors. The more pride, care, and positive use of the environment, the easier it is for a child to be in that space.

It's true that you can't judge the content and quality of a book by its cover, but an attractive cover is very helpful in getting people interested in buying it. It's the same with a classroom environment; in itself, appearance can't guarantee the content and quality of the education taking place, but it can be helpful in creating an interest, and providing a positive and attractive atmosphere that will be more likely to lead to your child receiving the best education possible.

You can learn much about what takes place in your child's classroom if you know what to look for and ask about in the environment. It can help you develop confidence in, or questions about, the education your child is receiving.

THE YEAR OF THE PET

When I teach, I always try to shape my classroom environment according to the needs, interests, and abilities of my class. One class was interested in writing and performing; another class always had different projects going. My favorite was 1967, the "Year of the Pet."

That year we had hamsters, gerbils, guinea pigs, a rabbit, a baby alligator, two iguanas, a couple of snakes, a large turtle, a bird, some chickens, an injured squirrel, and fish. The environment was dominated by pets—bulletin boards had stories, reports, and information about them; there were tanks and cages throughout the room; a play area was created where the pets were handled.

The spirit of the class was greatly enhanced by those pets, especially when the unexpected occurred. Once Leslie was doing math while Lizzy, the 1½-foot-long lizard, sat on his shoulder. In the middle of the classwork, Leslie shrieked as if attacked, and ran to the sink; you see Lizzy had "done her thing" on his shoulder. It was a funny moment.

Another time, Snowy, our chubby hamster, escaped from his cage and could not be found. We formed search parties and built traps, but after three days we gave up hope of finding him. Two weeks later we were walking down the hall when Mrs. Davis, who was sweeping under the radiators, screamed, dropped her broom, and stood frozen to the spot. There was Snowy, somewhat skinnier and much dirtier, running away. We all cheered as Darryl, Snowy's "keeper", ran and caught him.

Perhaps the "greatest moment" was the time our 2-foot-long garter snake disappeared. Each morning search parties entered the room before the class; then the children would look in their desks. Mrs. Davis, who normally took five minutes to sweep at 3 PM, managed to be in and out of my room in one-and-a-half minutes. Other teachers and their classes entered their rooms carefully and anxiously. When the snake was finally found under a shade four days later, there was much rejoicing throughout the school.

A rich, exciting, positively created classroom environment is something worth developing. It can help give class members a common interest, opportunities to learn firsthand, and pleasant, positive educational surroundings.

YOUR CHILD'S CLASSROOM ENVIRONMENT

You should know what to look for and ask about in your child's classroom. As you observe your child's classroom environment, keep the following questions in mind and decide which ones need to be answered by your child and/or the teacher:

1. How is the classroom environment helpful to my child's education?
2. Is the classroom intended for show or practical use?
3. Is it being used, and if so, is it used properly?
4. What is missing that should be in the classroom?
5. How could the environment be improved?
6. Does the room look appealing and attractive?
7. Is it a place in which you would like to spend anywhere from 45 minutes to 5 hours each day?

Structural Features of the Room

In your child's classroom, are there any broken or deteriorating features (shades, windows, light bulbs, desks, chairs, doors, chipped paint, and so on)? Is the lighting good? Check for glare and adequate illumination (see the section on lighting in Chapter Two, "The Home Study Learning Environment"). Is proper temperature and ventilation maintained? Check to see if the heaters work properly, if windows are in good working condition. Are there any hazards in the room, such as broken glass on a pet tank, sharp objects, wobbly chairs or desks?

Your Child's Work Space

Is your child's desk and/or chair the proper size and height? Is it comfortable? (See the section on posture in Chapter Two.) Is the study space properly located for your child's particular needs? (Can she see the board easily? Is there a vision or hearing problem that should cause the desk location to be changed?) Is the work space kept neat and organized or is it cluttered and disorganized?

You can find out the answers to these and other questions by talking with the teacher and your child and by visiting the classroom yourself.

Bulletin Boards

Bulletin boards are a valuable part of the classroom environment, but are often not properly used. They can and should be used to validate and motivate the work of children, as well as serving as a source of interesting and useful information and ideas.

The way bulletin boards are used can be a good indication of what goes on in the classroom—what types of things are emphasized (and not emphasized) by the teacher.

How much of the bulletin board display material is teacher-supplied and how much is the children's own work? What is the *variety* of children's material displayed? For example, is it only math and penmanship papers or compositions? Only art projects, or special reports? Or is there a good and interesting variety? Is the work of only a few or many children on display? How up to date is the displayed work? Sometimes the same papers or material can be up for months at a time (if so, ask the teacher about this—there may

be a valid reason). Is there special display material of interest and/or importance to the children (for example, basic math fact chart, the alphabet, reading posters)? How well-cared-for are the bulletin boards? Is the material neat and clearly displayed? Ask the teacher how he or she feels the bulletin boards can best be used and/or why they are used as they currently are.

Evidence of Children's Productiveness and Learning

It is very important that a child receive recognition for successes, and excellence. This is a great morale and pride booster. Find the ways a child's competence and success are shown and/or demonstrated in the classroom. To do this, look for such things as your child's work on bulletin boards; special projects and activities your child has completed or may be working on; your child's name on progress and/or achievement charts, graphs, or posters (these can help show how well your child is doing compared to others in the class).

Educational Material and Learning Aids

Observe what kind of educational materials are available in the classroom, and then find out why, how, and when the materials are used (and how helpful they are) by asking the teacher and your child. The material available (aids, kits, centers) for classes can give the impression that much is happening, when in reality it may not be used, or may be improperly used.

In many schools, classes share various material, so if you don't see some things you feel should be in the classroom, ask the teacher.

You should also check for additional learning aids. Is there a record player and various headset attachments so individuals or groups of children can listen without disturbing others? Is there a television set that can be used for educational programs? Are there cassette tape recorders; radios; filmstrip projector with accompanying filmstrips and recordings; movie projectors? At least some of these audiovisual aids should be present in your child's classroom. In addition, you should check for other learning aids such as various charts, posters, maps, globes, special teaching machines. Do you see any special equipment for science, math, art—such as bead frames, incubators, easels, and the like? Ask about other aids that may be used, but not currently in the room. Also check for reference materials, such as dictionaries and encyclopedias.

What type of instructional kits are available in the classroom for math, reading, science, social studies, and so forth? Are the kits for *instruction* or *enrichment* (to reinforce or practice things already learned)? What condition are the kits in—are they well organized, complete, in poor condition?

Check for Interest and Experience Centers

A good classroom environment should include some interest and experience centers. Does your child's class have any? What type are they? What is the purpose of each center? Are they all well cared for and organized? Is there evidence of use? If so, you'll find that the material is not *perfectly* new and clean. There may be charts and name lists indicating who's been using or is scheduled to use the center, or children actively working at the centers. Do you see completed projects being displayed?

Class Library

When a library is properly developed and utilized, it is an invaluable asset to any classroom. Does your child's classroom have a library? How is it organized? Are the books arranged at random, alphabetically by author or title, or by subject matter? Do the books seem appealing for children in the class? Check the titles, covers, subject matter, length of book, number of pictures, to get an idea of the type of books available.

How is the library used? Is there a checkout system, or are the books taken at random? Is the library an attractive area, set up as an interest center, or is it just books on shelves? Check with the teacher to see if the books are changed after a period of time. If they are, the children are more likely to use the library; if books aren't changed from time to time, the children will quickly lose interest.

Are the books written at different reading levels to allow for the various reading abilities of the children? (Books that are too easy can be just as much of a turnoff as the ones that are too hard.)

The Desk Arrangement

There are basically four types of desk arrangement, each having certain benefits and possible drawbacks.

The type of arrangement will depend on the philosophy of the teacher, the needs of a particular class or child, the type and number of desks available, and the limits determined by the room size and the equipment found in the room.

THINGS TO DO

◆ *Visit your child's classroom.* Be aware of its good points, bad points, and what's needed. Also, discuss with your child how she feels about the room (what she likes, doesn't like, would like to have different, and so on). You can also discuss with your child and the teacher what things you may have at home or can easily get that could be used in the classroom—for example, old book cases, an unused fish tank, old magazines.

◆ *During your visits to school (open school week and/or night), compare your child's classroom with other rooms.* Observe what other rooms in the school have that your child's doesn't, and vice versa.

◆ *Communicate with the school staff and other parents.* Particularly if you are displeased with the classroom environment, make sure you discuss this with your child's teacher, the administrator, and if possible, other parents. One aim of these discussions should be to find out what can be done to improve the classroom environment.

chapter 6

You and Your Child's Teacher

BASIC VIEWPOINT

The greater your expressed interest, concern, and involvement for your child's schooling, the greater the teacher's (and school's) active interest and concern will be.

It's easy to find excuses to avoid communicating with your child's teacher.

"I'm too busy—my schedule is too hectic."
"They know what they're doing."
"Who am I to butt in? I don't know enough."
"I'm too tired."
"The traffic is too heavy to walk two blocks."
"Once he's in school, my child is *their* concern, not mine."

These are only a few of the reasons that parents give for not actively involving themselves with their child's teacher(s) and school.

There are so many children to deal with that teachers and other school personnel find it extremely difficult to provide the optimum time, energy, help, and instruction each child needs and deserves. But when you as a parent express interest, concern, and involvement (or pressure, if that's what is needed to get things moving), the teachers and school personnel—recognizing how much progress can be made by a child with proper parental help—will be likely to give more attention and active interest to your child.

In addition, some teachers and other school personnel will take a more active interest in children whose parents have insisted the school meet their child's needs, if only to avoid upsetting and having to confront those angry parents.

As you read this chapter, keep in mind that the expectations you have and the way you work with your child's teacher will vary according to where your child is—in elementary school, junior high, or high school. The nature of the teacher's role will vary considerably within different school-level situations.

Elementary school teachers generally have more of an overall involvement in your child's education and will be responsible for from twenty to thirty children. Junior high and high school teachers have a more limited involvement to one subject area, and are usually responsible for a great many more students.

THE BIGGEST LIVING PARENT

My friend Dave told me of a rather unexpected parent-teacher conference he had one day.

He was restively eating lunch alone in his room, when suddenly the biggest living parent he'd ever seen appeared in his doorway. The parent, child in hand, glared at Dave and in a very unloving voice asked, *"Why did you choke my child?"*

As the parent approached, Dave knew he'd better quickly establish good communication with this angry parent, or he was in for real trouble.

Dave stood up and stretched all of his thin 6'4" frame as

high as he could and said, as he gulped his food, "Let me explain."

The parent moved closer and asked in a more menacing tone, "Why did you choke my child?"

Dave's next words were enough to deflect the parent's obvious intention to commit mayhem on his body. He looked at the child, who was quietly standing next to his parent and asked, "Why did you say I choked you? That never happened. Did you tell what really took place?"

Fifteen minutes of Dave sighing with relief and a discussion about what actually happened followed. Dave had broken up a fight between the boy and another child and had had to pull his student off the other child. It seems the boy had been recently involved in a number of fights that Dave had never reported to the parent. After hearing the full story the parent was more than willing to work with Dave to help handle the problem.

Dave was careful to never do anything that would antagonize that parent, especially by indifference or lack of communication on his part. The parent realized how "jumping to conclusions" is not as helpful as "walking to the truth," and that it is important to really find out the facts of a situation before acting.

Parent-teacher relations are a vital aspect of a child's school survival. What follows are some things you should be aware of regarding those relationships.

COMMUNICATION BETWEEN PARENT AND TEACHER

The communication between teacher and parent is vital. At the beginning of the school year, you should let the teacher know that you expect to be in touch with her (or him) and to maintain close contact with the school throughout the year.

This initial communication will go a long way in establishing a positive relationship in which you'll support the teacher's efforts in your child's behalf.

Teachers can communicate with parents in many ways: through regular newsletters describing what's occurring or what will occur in the class; regular conferences with parents; small or large group meetings; seminars; phone calls; home visits; invitations for class visits; messages delivered by your child; chance meetings as you pick up or deliver your child; regular report cards.

There should be a regular communication line between parent and teacher, with teachers using easily understood language, not educational jargon.

Among the things a teacher should communicate to the parents are: the general way the class is being organized and run; how well your child is progressing academically, socially, and emotionally; what things are going well, what areas need improvement; specific pointers on how you can help your child's progress; response to any questions or concerns you have voiced; general information on things you should be aware of (class trips, special meetings, and the like); the actual educational program the school/teacher is developing.

When you receive a communication about your child from a teacher, you should separate fact from opinion. Any opinion expressed about your child should be backed up with specific information, or it won't be very helpful. For example, if the teacher writes only "Your child is lazy," you have no helpful or relevant information to explain this opinion.

A more helpful statement from the teacher would be, "Your child is lazy. He starts his work 5 minutes after everyone else, does no extra-credit work, and has only completed two of his last eight assignments." Though the information does not necessarily indicate that your child is *lazy* (he could be bored, angry, confused about the work he's to do), it is useful for understanding the basis of the teacher's opinion.

It's up to you to read, understand, and evaluate a

teacher's communication, and to request further information if and as it is needed.

Don't forget—teachers enjoy receiving communications from parents that are positive about the work they're doing with your child. Get in touch with your child's teacher when things are going well, not just when there's some problem.

Parent-Teacher Conferences

Conferences can be called for many reasons: to develop a good working relationship, to report general progress, or to deal with specific situations. Conferences provide a time to give, receive, and share ideas and information that will help your child.

There are several things you should expect to find out from a parent-teacher conference:

1. What are your child's needs and strengths—academically, socially, and emotionally? The teacher should provide specific, concrete examples, such as the child's grades, the work folder, anecdotal records giving detailed accounts of relevant incidents that have occurred (both good and bad).
2. What is being done to help handle the needs of your child, and what is being done to use and develop your child's strengths and abilities?
3. What specific things can you do to help your child's progress in school, generally, or in selected areas such as reading, developing work habits, art, and so forth?
4. What are the names of other relevant school personnel you can talk to about your child's progress in school (principal, medical staff, gym instructor)?

In addition, you should express your concerns and interests to the teacher and relate any information that will bring about a better understanding of your child's needs, interests, abilities, and potential. It is helpful to list the things you want to know or discuss about your child's schooling *before* you go to the conference.

The conference is a good time to establish a meaningful working relationship with your child's teacher. Communicate what you expect and want for your child's education, and how you are prepared to help.

In the third year I was teaching I had several parents who were very active and insistent about getting what they expected from me and the school. They strongly urged that I give extra work and activities to their children.

At first I was a bit angered that parents would dare tell me, the *teacher*, what I should teach my class. I did not feel that what they were asking was really that important for their children. After talking further with the parents, though, I realized that they had every right to expect and even demand that I provide what they believed was essential for their children. It was my job to either convince them otherwise, arrange to have their expectations met, or recommend that their children be placed in a different class or school where their demands could best be met.

Remember, it's *your child*. Be willing to communicate and work with the teacher to see that what you feel is important will happen. Be supportive, helpful, and cooperative, but also be insistent that the needs of your child be met. *Hold the teacher responsible.* Your child's future and happiness is at stake.

Don't be intimidated by the teacher, or by any school personnel—they are really working for you. You help pay their salary, and your child's education is the focus of the school situation.

I know what it is like to be intimidated by teachers. When I began teaching, I could not bring myself to call any of the older teachers by their first names. Those over 40 (old to me at the time, but certainly not now as I approach my fortieth birthday), I called Mr.____ or Mrs.____ during my first full year of teaching. The second year was better. I called them Mr. M. or Mrs. L., using last name initials when I addressed them. I finally overcame the intimidation from my past experiences with teachers, and in my third year of teaching it was easy to use first names. It took *me* almost 5 years of teaching to get used to being called *Mr.* Percy without feeling intimidated by myself.

EVALUATING YOUR CHILD'S TEACHER

Does your child have a good teacher? There is perhaps no more important or difficult question to answer concerning his schooling. Your child's education turns and depends on the ability and effectiveness of his teachers. It's for you to judge whether or not your child's teacher is good. For this you need criteria to use in your evaluation.

This next section will present information and viewpoints to help you establish criteria for judging a teacher's effectiveness.

Understand What It Means To Be a Teacher

In all fairness, when you evaluate a teacher you should keep in mind the nature of a teacher's work with the many responsibilities and things to consider and handle:

> Twenty to thirty children, each with his or her own abilities, needs, talents, problems, and potentials (in junior high and high school a teacher may have 150 or more students)

Twenty to thirty sets of parents to work with, consider, and try to please (in junior high and high school the numbers are far greater)

Certain expectations and requirements set forth by the school board, district superintendent, principal, and any other supervisor to whom the teacher is responsible

Sometimes the teacher has a union contract to abide by

Personal abilities, interests, problems, needs, and potentials each teacher brings to a class

The necessity to plan and implement valid plans for a program and an environment in which children can learn and expand to their full potential

Personal beliefs that may conflict with what they are required to and/or pressured to do

It is especially important to recognize the difficulty a teacher often has when it comes to satisfying the needs and wants of parents. You as a parent have viewpoints and concerns about your child's education. And it is not uncommon for these to be the opposite of other parents' desires and concerns. In addition, your viewpoints may be opposed by official school policy, or the teacher's personal feelings and beliefs.

Direct Observation

One of the best methods to use in determining the effectiveness of your child's teacher is to observe her or his work with your child's class. There are things you can look for that will help give you a better understanding of how good and effective the teacher is. Among the areas to consider are academics, human relations, teaching style, and classroom organization.

Academics involves the teacher's ability to motivate and help your child learn the subject matter your child needs to, wants to, and is trying to know and understand.

To determine the effectiveness of a teacher's academic program, you can ask the following questions:

> How well are the three basic study principles discussed in Chapter Four utilized by the teacher?
> How knowledgeable is the teacher about the subject matter?
> How well prepared is the teacher in terms of knowing and presenting the material in a clear, understandable way?
> How ready is the teacher to handle a variety of students' responses and needs?

How much evidence is there of students' successes, gains, accomplishments, and good morale during the time you observe?

Human relations involves the teacher's ability to get along with and handle individual children, a small group, or the entire class, and how well the teacher helps the children work and relate with each other.

To determine the effectiveness of a teacher's human relations ability, look for answers to these questions:

How well does the teacher communicate with the class? Is there a give and take of viewpoints during discussion, or is what the teacher says and thinks basically accepted and done?

Is there a feeling of respect for the children? Or is the feeling more like tolerance, with an attitude that seems to say, "Kids are not people"?

Do the children seem to be at ease when they actively participate with the teacher in some activity?

What is the general feeling of the class (fearful, relaxed, active, passive, happy, angry, good morale, bad morale)?

How respectful, helpful, and cooperative are the children with each other?

How much interaction among the children is allowed and motivated by the teacher?

How well has the teacher instilled in the children a sense of respect and recognition that she is the *teacher*, and do the children understand what their responsibilities are to the teacher, themselves, and the other children in class?

Teaching style and classroom organization concerns the way a teacher sets up and runs the class. These factors greatly influence the mood, feeling, and structure of the class environment. What follows is a brief description of some of the more common types of classroom organization.

The two basic grouping patterns used by schools are

called *heterogeneous* and *homogeneous*. These patterns are also used in the organization of groups within each class.

In *heterogeneous* grouping, a class is set up with children of varying degrees and levels of achievement. Most heterogeneous groups are based on academic achievement levels. Such things as personality, cooperativeness, maturity, attitude, behavior, and effort may also be taken into account in the creation of a heterogeneous class or group.

In a *homogeneous* group, children of basically similar levels of ability and/or academic achievement are placed in one class. Attitude, maturity, behavior, and other personality considerations are generally less important in deciding who goes into a homogeneously organized group or class.

In the *traditional self-contained classroom*, the teacher is responsible for the overall education of a specific group of children. The teacher plans the educational program, generally using established curriculum guides for the age and grade level of the class taught. The particular needs and interests of the class are also considered, with learning and interest centers helping to meet and handle the specific needs and interests of the students.

The *open classroom* is a setting in which a child is encouraged to assume much of the responsibility for his learning, behavior, purposes, and attitudes. The child works at a self-determined pace, choosing the activities to study and get involved with. There may be separate activity areas for math, reading, science, and so forth. The activities of the centers change according to the child's needs, interests, and purposes.

A teacher in the open classroom must be aware of what the children are doing; work with individual children or small or large groups depending on the needs, abilities, and interests of the students; develop and plan challenging activities; and direct students' attention to the appropriate activities.

The *nongraded* classroom has children of various ages. The class emphasizes the need and importance of children progressing at their own rate and not being pushed ahead too quickly, or slowed down unnecessarily because of where the rest of the group is. Children in an ungraded class move from one level to another as their particular interest, readiness, and ability level changes.

In this type of class, there is a recognition that children progress at varying speeds in different areas of the school curriculum. For example, a single child may be equal to a 9-year-old in reading, a 6-year-old in math, and a 10-year-old in physical dexterity.

Team or *cooperative teaching* occurs when teachers share responsibilities for teaching a specific group of children. They decide—depending on their particular skills and interests— how, what, and who to teach during the school day.

Departmentalization is usually found in junior high and high schools, in which classes are organized on a subject basis. Each teacher is responsible for teaching a particular subject to a group of children. The children move from room to room according to their subjects.

Flexible grouping and scheduling are found in a classroom in which several approaches are used to organize a class. Here the teacher uses what he or she feels most comfortable with, and/or whatever approach is best for the students.

Discuss with your child's teacher what type of organization is being used, and *why* that particular type of organization is being used. Ask your child what he likes and doesn't like about the system. Observe how the physical surroundings of the room contribute to the method of instruction used by the teacher. For example, in an open classroom look at the interest centers, paying special attention to how provisions are made for children of different ability levels within similar areas of interest. In a traditional class you might look at the provisions made for individual interests.

The *teacher's style*, in addition to the way she or he

organizes the class, will be a major factor in how well your child succeeds in and enjoys school. Look for such things as the teacher's poise, enthusiasm, responsiveness and receptiveness to the needs of the children, general approach to teaching (warm and accepting or stern and authoritative).

Very importantly, observe whether the teacher tends to conduct the class like a lecture, doing just about all the talking, with little listening and active supervision, or more in the manner of a guide, putting the students' attention on certain things and motivating them to find out more for themselves, actively supervising and observing the progress of the children, and listening carefully to students' reactions and ideas.

SCHOOL'S INFLUENCE ON TEACHER EFFECTIVENESS

The teacher is part of a whole organization and to varying degrees her or his success is dependent on the policies, programs, personnel, working conditions, and materials of that organization. To measure the effectiveness of your child's teacher you really have to consider and understand the type of support (or lack of it) the school provides.

Teachers have areas of special interest, talents, and expertise. They also have areas in which their competence is not as good and in which they need added support and help. To be as effective as possible, the classroom teacher has to rely on the knowledge and abilities of the rest of the school staff, including supervisors, other teachers, guidance counselors, school nurse, specially-trained teachers from the school district, the custodial staff, school volunteers, and parents. In addition, the availability, condition, and use of various supplies, materials, and facilities helps determine how effective the teacher can be.

The importance of a school principal's support in helping a teacher become more effective cannot be underestimated. Though the principal has certain school district guidelines to follow, he or she helps establish the priorities of the school, decides how to utilize various personnel, determines how resources and facilities of the school can be used, and influences the type of classroom organization and to some extent the teaching style of the teacher. The principal's leadership establishes the climate and tone of the school.

I saw firsthand how important a principal's influence can be. In one inner-city school, where I enjoyed my occasional substituting assignments, there was a wonderful environment, for both teachers and students. At this school the children came up to the room from the schoolyard *unescorted* by their teacher—almost unheard of in the inner city. I looked forward to my days there.

After summer vacation I was asked to substitute for a day at the school, which I gladly agreed to do. When I arrived, I was instantly aware of a dramatic change—for the worse. Without asking anyone, I knew what had occurred. There was a new principal. The climate of the school was markedly different than the year before. The children were more disruptive and disorderly, staff morale was down, and the school was a less effective institution of learning. The new principal disregarded or changed many of the successful actions of the former principal, to the detriment of the school. I rarely accepted offers to work in that school again.

When you walk into a school, *feel* it. Observe the facilities (the gymnasium, auditorium, lunchroom, yard, offices). Watch how the children relate to each other, and to the teachers; how the teachers relate to the children and to other teachers. See how well-maintained the building is. Peek into classes as you walk to your child's room. How welcomed do you feel by the office staff, teachers, and supervisors? In this way you will be in touch with a principal's leadership.

THINGS TO DO

◆ *Some questions to ask when evaluating your child's teacher:*

1. What is your child's attitude toward the teacher and the school?
2. What changes have you noticed (both good and bad) in your child that you can trace back to his teacher?
3. What does your child say about his teacher? (Be aware that if your child is critical of his teacher it can indicate the teacher's inability to work successfully with your child, *or* it can indicate that your child has not been meeting his class and/or school responsibilities, and defends his failures by unfairly criticizing his teacher. Don't jump to conclusions—get more information from the teacher, other parents, students, and anyone else familiar with the situation. Then decide what is really happening.)
4. How closely does the teacher meet the needs of your child (as you understand and believe them to be)?
5. How is your child doing academically?
6. Is your child learning things he can use to better his schooling and life?
7. Is the teacher very specific in discussing your child, or very general?
8. How communicative and responsive is the teacher toward you?
9. What does the classroom environment tell you about the teacher?
10. What do other people, whose opinion you respect, say about the teacher?

11. How close does the teacher come to meeting your expectations of what your child's teacher should be, do, and have?

12. Add any other questions you feel are relevant.

◆ *Make lists that will help you evaluate and work with your child's teacher.*

Expectations for My
Child's Teacher

> I expect my child's teacher to:

send home both good and bad notes.
come to school on time with few absences.
control the class.
emphasize the use of good and effective study skills.
create and maintain a warm, creative working environment.
keep me informed about what's happening in class.
insist on keeping a neat and pleasant environment.
find time to work with each child individually every day.
stress basics of reading, math, and science.
help develop and cultivate new interests and awarenesses in my child.
work with my child when he gets a failing, or a poor mark, and not just give him a grade and forget it.

Needs and Priorities of
My Child

> My child needs:

a lot of exposure to the arts.
a strict, no-nonsense teacher/a giving, relaxed teacher.
help in starting assignments and activities.
help in becoming more organized about his work.

work on reading comprehension skills.

preparation for a technical school.

(Add items according to your child's needs.)

Helpful Information for
the Teacher

My child:

has a special talent for art.

tends to give up if harshly criticized.

can't stay late because he has to pick up his sister.

has a strong interest in astronomy.

◆ *Figure out how you can best help your child's teacher.*   Ask
the teacher what is needed and wanted, specifically for your
child, and generally for the class. Based on your schedule,
talents, interests, and knowledge, decide how you could make
a meaningful contribution. For example, perhaps you could
supply some materials the class needs; teach a lesson on a
topic you know very well; be a class parent on a trip; tutor a
group of children after school.

◆ *Meet your child's teacher.*   Very often, parents are
reluctant to meet with the teacher in the school. If this is the
case, there are many alternative ways of organizing a parent-
teacher conference. One effective method for opening up
communication between parents and teacher is an after-
school meeting at a parent's house. Parents tend to be more
relaxed in a home setting.

You can also meet with other parents and discuss various
ways of fostering parent-teacher meetings and cooperation.
Reread the relevant section of the chapter on parent-teacher
conferences before meeting with your child's teacher, and
prepare questions, lists, information, or whatever you feel is
necessary.

◆ *What if you want your child's teacher changed?* There are several points you should consider if you think your child should switch teachers. Why do you think the change is necessary? Do you have valid reasons, or have you decided because of hearsay and rumor? Make very sure you make such a decision based on your own careful observation and investigation of the situation.

Then you must decide whether or not there is a better teacher or learning situation for your child. Another important consideration is your child's own feelings about having his class changed.

Is there any way of working with the teacher to improve the situation? Perhaps the change isn't really necessary. If it is, you should be prepared with pertinent information for the school principal. Be very sure it is the right decision—one that will help your child.

chapter 7

Drugs and Alcohol — The Wrong Solution to Any Problem

BASIC VIEWPOINT

Alcohol and drugs are *not* the problem, but are basically the wrong *solution* to any problem that a person might have. Help your child decide on her own not to use drugs.*

Police report that the drug abuse problem has grown to epidemic proportions; there are an estimated 1⅓ million alcoholics between the ages of 12 and 17; many children are being admitted to mental institutions because of their involvement with drugs and alcohol.** And in the 1977 Gallup Poll of public attitudes toward public schools, the primary concern of parents was what to do about drugs, smoking, and alcohol.

Drug and alcohol abuse problems have no societal, racial, or geographical boundary; they are a festering wound that

*I would like to especially acknowledge two people for their help in preparing this chapter: *Adele Rosse*, Executive Director of Right Track (an organization that uses celebrities to help children stay on the right track to the future by educating them about the actual effects of drugs and helps youngsters decide for themselves not to be on drugs) and *Greg Zerovnik*, a former director of Narconon (a very effective drug rehabilitation program), ex-drug user and dealer, now a successful business and management consultant.

**Data reported to Right Track, Hollywood, California.

infects individual children, their families, and society, wreaking destruction on the quality of a child's life and ability to successfully cope and survive. This is a problem we must all be aware of, confront, and handle.

EVERYBODY'S PROBLEM

If you look around at your family, friends, and/or associates, chances are good that you will find examples of drug and alcohol abuse that are, or have been, destructive.

I have personally observed the ravages of alcohol and drug use and abuse. I've known students whose life revolved around alcohol and/or drugs; some were pushing, others were using; some were dying. One was murdered because of drugs; another tried to commit suicide; and far too many became nonproductive leeches of society.

Drug and alcohol abuse is indeed everybody's problem.

WHY CHILDREN USE DRUGS AND ALCOHOL

Finding out why children use drugs and alcohol is the most fundamental step in preventing and/or handling drug and alcohol abuse. In my research and discussions with various authorities—including parents, children, current and former drug users and heavy drinkers—many reasons were given for the use and abuse, some more basic than others. Among them were the following:

Low self-esteem

Inability to make reasonable decisions

To escape situations and problems

Belief that drugs are not harmful

Inquisitiveness and experimentation

Belief that meaningful awareness, change and understanding must come from sources outside oneself

No real purpose to life (no activity—music, art, sports—that helps make her feel good, satisfied, and/or competent)

For fun

Belief that drugs make one feel good (A friend of mine, an ex-druggie and dealer, told me about giving people phony pills and watching them show all the effects of being on real drugs; he stated, "the drug was an *excuse* to do things they wouldn't ordinarily do and experience.")

Peer pressure ("Use it or you're not part of the group, punk!")

Suppression of physical pain

Substitution of television viewing for real experiences; drugs continue the pattern of substituting for the real experiences a child has not had or feels she can't really get for herself

"Everybody does it, so it must be ok"

Parental use of drugs, both legal and illegal, to handle their life situations and problems

Commercial advertisement of drugs; children are bombarded with hype that drugs will make us feel good and handle tension, headaches, upsets, and other unwanted feelings

Belief that drugs will better her life so she can *be* more, *do* more, and *have* more

Addiction to drugs or alcohol can cause physical dependence to develop, especially for alcohol, sedatives (including tranquilizers and sleeping pills), and narcotics; psychological dependence develops; or both physical and psychological dependence develop

All these reasons are basically wrong solutions to any problems that a person might have.

IS MY CHILD TAKING DRUGS?

A friend of mine related this story about how she discovered that her son was smoking marijuana.

She has a wonderful, open, warm relationship with her 14-year-old son, who is very creative and does exceptionally well at school. One day the mother of her son's best friend called to say she suspected their sons were smoking pot together and suggested, "You'd better search Steve's room to see if he's got any."

My friend was shocked—how could this be? She had always communicated to her son her strong belief that marijuana provides an artificial high—that true highs come naturally from life and are ones you give yourself. She also expressed her concern about the physically damaging effects that pot (and other drugs) might have on the body.

For the first time in her life, she felt that she had to search her son's room; she did not feel particularly proud about the search, but felt it necessary. Sure enough—she found the marijuana. She immediately called a friend who was familiar with the drug scene. He came by and verified that it was indeed pot.

Later that day she confronted her son, and told him what had occurred that day. She asked why he was using pot. His response was, "To experience what it was like; I was just experimenting, Mom."

How You Can Find Out If Your Child Is Taking Drugs

It is very difficult for a parent to discover drug use in the case of a child who is only a casual user—one who is basically experimenting. The heavier user, especially one who is addicted to drugs or alcohol, is much easier to spot.

Please understand that the following signs are only indications that drugs or alcohol *may* be used by your child. Do not jump to conclusions, and do not assume there is a drug problem if you find some of the following things happening with your child. Things other than drugs could be contributing to what you observe. If you suspect drug or alcohol use, confront your child with your findings and find out what's happening. When you confront your child, don't do it with an attitude of condemnation and harassment. Instead, make it clear that your involvement is out of love and concern, and that you want to know what you can do to help.

Some General Things to Look For

A change in routine and lifestyle For example; your child may come home later, leave earlier. She may sleep much longer hours; stay out all night and sleep during the day; have different friends and hang out in different places than before.

Important attitude and behavior changes For example; although usually calm and placid, your child may suddenly become grumpy and irritable. A usually active and outgoing child may become apathetic, with a "who cares?" type of attitude. From being neat and careful, she may become sloppy and careless. She may be less able to concentrate and may seem blank and incoherent at times.

Sudden mood shifts For example: Your child may go from a calm state to one that is upset and irritable very quickly, and for no apparent reason. She may become unusually critical, even irrational, in outbursts of irritability.

Paraphernalia For example: you may find syringes, bogus prescriptions (used for pharmaceutical quality drugs), empty gelatin capsules, aspirin bottles with no aspirins in them, but a pill that has a different or no brand name.

Generally withdrawn and antisocial behavior

Physical changes and characteristics For example: your childs eyes may appear glossy, speech tends to slur. She may look run-down, with weight loss. Her face may look flushed, with pupils unusually constricted.

Things generally not going well and getting worse For example: you may notice a sudden dropoff in grades; your child may cut classes. Usual activities that involved and interested her no longer do, and no apparent new ones take their place. She may be getting into trouble at home, school, or in the neighborhood.

Frequent requests for money, or money and household items missing

A "gut" feeling that something is wrong with your child

There will be degrees of effects upon your child, depending on the type of drug, its potency, how often and how much is used; the child's physical and psychological well-being and reaction to the drug; the cause and purpose of your child's using the drug; the circumstances and environment involved in the drug use.

One of the effects of using drugs and/or alcohol is the damage it does to your child's school experience. How can a child perform well in school if she can't concentrate and keep attention on work, if she is too tired to stay awake, if her attendance suffers, if she has no purpose for studying because her purposes center around drugs?

THE EFFECTS OF DRUGS AND ALCOHOL

Before reading the chart on pages 116–18, there are two points I want to stress:

1. Drugs affect different people differently.
2. Drugs don't necessarily cause a user to act in a certain

way. They may set in motion a tendency, or pattern of action and behavior, that already exists in the user, but may be otherwise suppressed.

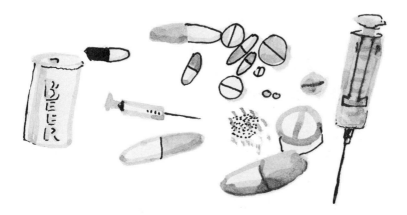

It is important to stress that if you notice what may be patterns of drug- or alcohol-related behavior and effects, find out the truth and don't *assume* you know for certain what's happening. There's a play on the word "assume" that I feel is appropriate. "Assume" makes an "ass" (of) *u* (and) *me*. It's easy to jump to conclusions, but wiser to walk to the truth.

Discuss the situation with your child, not with condemnation, anger, or bitterness, but with a sincere desire to know what's happening.

PREVENTION OF DRUG USE

It's helpful to remind you here that drug use isn't the problem, but the *wrong solution* to a problem. It's up to you as a parent to educate your child about drugs and to try to

Table 7-1 Effects of Various Drugs and Alcohol*

Type of Drug	Examples of Drug	Noticeable Effects While Taking Drug May Include:	Noticeable Effects of Habitual Use of Drug May Include:
SEDATIVES (Medical use is to help quiet and relax; tends to induce sleepiness.)	*Barbiturates:* Seconal, Tuinal, etc. (highly addictive) *Hypnotics:* Quaaludes, Sopor, etc. *Tranquilizers:* Valium, Miltown, Librium, etc.	Symptoms similar to intoxication—slurred speech, lack of coordination, confused thinking, looks sleepy, pupils constricted, feeling of well-being and relaxation.	Serious mental illness, impaired memory, slurred speech, irritability, lack of coordination, dulled reactions.
STIMULANTS (Medical use is to elevate spirits; makes one more alert; in large doses it excites the user.)	*Amphetamines:* Ritalin, Dexedrine, Benzedrine, etc.	Dilated pupils, rapid speech, excitability, loss of appetite, false sense of pep and mental alertness, nervousness, fever, irritability, dizziness, sweating, loss of coordination, aggressive, talkative.	Insomnia, restlessness, malnutrition and weight loss, fatigue, paranoia, sudden violent acts, irritability, loss of mental powers.
NARCOTICS (Medical use is to lessen pain.)	*Heroin, Methadone, Morphine, Opium,* and *Opium Derivatives:* Codeine, Demerol, Paregoric, etc. (all narcotics are highly addictive)	Tranquil, euphoric feeling, sluggishness, drowsiness, loss of appetite and physical energy, constricted pupils, watery eyes, itchiness, sweaty, runny nose, nodding (drowsiness and wakening state alternate—not aware of the environment), slurred speech.	Weight loss, overall breakdown in health, possible tracks and needle marks (also see symptoms in column to left).

HALLUCINOGENS (Psychedelics.)	LSD, Mescaline, Peyote, etc.	*Hallucinations* (sensing things not found in the environment—e.g., hearing a sound no one else hears). *Illusions* (misinterpreting reality—e.g., seeing an insect and thinking it's a dinosaur), panic, fear, dilated pupils, incoherent speech, sudden mood shifts, flushed face, disconnected speech (talk on a topic, then trail out and start new one before completing the first topic).	*Flashbacks* (sensations of a drug experience that happened in the past), depression, anxiety, thinking, judgment, and perception may be distorted.
CANNABIS	Marijuana, Hashish	Reddened eyes, lessening of anxieties, euphoria, lowered motivation, increased appetite (especially for sweets), intoxication, lightheadedness, lessening of inhibitions, distinctive odor (something like burned alfalfa hay).	Loss of energy and drive, slow confused thinking, lack of interest in activity.
COCAINE (Medical use is to alleviate pain)	Cocaine	Dilated pupils, elation, euphoria, appetite loss, appears intoxicated.	Damage to nasal membranes, marked weight loss.
PCP (Angel Dust.)	PCP	Illusions, hallucinations, lack of coordination, flushed face, watering eyes, mental confusion.	Flashbacks, anxiety, depression.

INHALANTS	Aerosols, Paint Thinner, Airplane Glue, Gasoline, etc.	Dilated pupils, dizziness, lack of coordination, drowsiness, slurred speech, euphoria, impaired reaction and judgment, nausea, vomiting, hangover the next day (nausea, headache, shakiness, and possibly vomiting), coughing, sneezing, distinctive odor of glue, etc.	Nosebleeds, bloodshot eyes, fatigue, weight loss, irritability, forgetfulness, sores on nose and mouth, tremors, hostility.
ALCOHOL	Beer, Wine, Liquor	Uninhibited behavior, the odor of alcohol, lack of coordination, drowsiness, slurred speech, impaired reaction and judgment, nausea, vomiting, dizziness, hangover the next day.	Loss of memory, blackouts, hangovers.

*(Note: the effects vary greatly, depending on the dose of the particular drug, its strength, the circumstances under which it is taken, and the individual's physical and psychological condition.)

prevent problems that could lead to drug use as an attempted solution. In the sections following we will discuss three basic steps you can take to prevent your child from turning to drugs.

Educate Your Child about Drugs

Help your child recognize and understand the effects of taking drugs. There are many information programs and materials prepared by various groups and organizations that you and your child's school can and should be using. Find out about your child's knowledge of and attitudes toward drugs. What is her school doing in terms of drug education? (You will find references concerning drug information and program sources in the "Things to Do" section of this chapter).

Here are some key points to remember when you are educating your child about drugs:

1. Don't try to impose your viewpoints. Don't invalidate or put down your child's ideas, especially in an antagonistic tone. That will quickly cause your child to defend her viewpoints, making it much harder for the truth to be looked at, especially during adolescence, during which, in Adele Rosse's words, "self-determination is parading around as rebellion."

2. Present facts to help clear up misunderstandings and misconceptions about drugs. Use whatever sources and materials are appropriate for your child.

3. Label opinions as opinions. If you label opinion as fact and your child discovers viewpoints that reasonably contradict your absolute truth, your credibility will suffer.

4. Try to present your ideas, viewpoints, and facts in a positive way—one your child can relate to. Adele Rosse gives a very successful example of this approach.
   An example that never fails to hit home is the saga of

the new car. "How many of you would like to have your own car," I'll ask. Ooooooooos and Aaaaaaaaaahs are punctuated with the swift shots of hands to the ceiling.

I then ask them to individually describe their dream machines. I get the children to imagine that they have it, own it, and are now driving it (they really like this part).

Now I say, "Let's pretend that I'm your good friend, and I tell you that you should fill the gas tank with orange juice. Would you do it?" (Boy, do I get booed at that point. So I retaliate.) "But why not, orange juice is cheaper and if I'm your friend and I tell you, then you should do it, right?"

To really get the steam off, I'll let them tell me why they wouldn't do it. Then I throw in the clincher. "What if I think you're dumb if you won't do it?" Only on rare occasions does anyone back down at this point.

That leaves me in a perfect position to say, "Well, if you feel that way about your car, why don't you feel that way about your self and your body? Don't forget, it's a lot easier to get a new car than it is to get a new body."

Somehow this drives the point home without making anyone wrong for decisions they've made.

5. Utilize your child's opinion leaders to deliver the no-drug-use message. These opinion leaders can be celebrities, family members, friends, authority figures—anyone your child respects, looks up to, and will listen to.

6. Don't be hypocritical. For example, if you discuss how important it is to face up to life, and use your own abilities and talents for success without falling back on drugs or alcohol, and then you proceed to pop a tranquilizer or take a couple of stiff drinks to handle some personal upset or problem, what do you expect your child to believe?

Help Your Child Be Active and Successful

Greg Zerovnik says, "Drugs involve lifestyle. A constructive lifestyle, in which the kids are active in life, leads to less chance for a destructive lifestyle in which they become heavily addicted."

Adele Rosse states, "Encouragement in activities of any kind are deterrents to getting sidetracked by drugs. From all the reports I've gotten from local police, the kids who are involved in activities, and especially the ones who are on "health kicks," are the ones who will stay away from drugs."

She continues, "Both Erik Estrada and Lawrence Hilton Jacobs [well-known actors who are members of Right Track] grew up in Harlem. There were drugs being used all around them. Neither one of them got into drugs because 'they didn't have time.' They were both too busy with activities—music, art, acting, sports—to ever get into drugs. Interestingly enough, they both speak about a loving family; they grew up with a sense of encouragement and a strong feeling of knowing what they wanted, and enjoyed going after it.".

Ms. Rosse suggests, "A good project for your family is to find out what your children enjoy doing. List things they like to do, things they want to learn, and then set aside time for those things to be accomplished."

Help Your Child Develop Self-Esteem and Decision-Making Ability

Self-esteem and ability to make decisions will, of course, influence many aspects of your child's life, including performance in school and the way she deals with situations in which there may be opportunities to use drugs.

The subject of helping develop a child's self-esteem is covered in Chapter One, *"How to Develop Good Work Habits."*

One of my former students, Ann Arthur, wrote, "A child has to learn to be independent. Prepare your child to stand on her own two feet. Parents won't always be with their child to show them right from wrong. A child has to learn to make decisions."*

* Bernard Percy, ed., *How To Grow A Child . . . A Child's Advice To Parents* (Los Angeles: Price, Stern & Sloan Publishers, Inc., 1978), p. 24.

There are two aspects related to decision making that you should consider: a child must have self-esteem and successful experiences in having made decisions, including learning from mistakes and wrong decisions; and a child needs to develop the ability to make the best decision for a problem or situation—that is, a decision that will lead to the greatest good. For this, she must have opportunities to evaluate (individually and with others) the decisions she has made, and must be able to decide between alternative choices, and then keep to that decision.

To develop the decision-making ability of your child, find and use opportunities that are appropriate to her situation, age, needs, and capabilities. For example, you can ask your toddler which pair of socks she wants to wear; let your 5-year-old decide if she wants to play in the park or ride her bike; let your 9-year-old decide whether or not to take a raincoat to school. Have your 12-year-old decide how she would like to earn her allowance.

Let your child experience some of the bumps, frustrations, and failures of growing up. Help her handle them and learn from them. Don't become so overprotective that you end up making all the decisions for your child, and have her rely on you for everything.

I think a poem written by Reggie Wright for the book *How To Grow A Child* is appropriate at this point. He wrote:

Oh my Lord, for goodness sake
I won't let you make this mistake
I did the same thing when I was a child
Then I cried for a week and my mom went wild
Please don't do this and don't do that
Cause you'll get hurt, and that's a fact!*

If your child knows the truth about drugs, has meaningful activities in which she is actively involved, and has the self-

* Percy, *How To Grow A Child*, p. 22

esteem and ability to make her own decisions, then the chances that she will become a drug user will be significantly decreased.

WHAT TO DO IF YOUR CHILD IS USING DRUGS

If you find out that your child is taking drugs, there are several things you can do. Find someone (yourself, a family member, friend, teacher) with whom she can talk—someone she can trust.

Find out the exact nature of the drug use. If your child has developed a physical and/or psychological dependence on drugs, find out what type of drug(s) are being used, how much, and how often. When (under what emotional and/or environmental circumstance) does your child use drugs? Where does she use drugs? What are her feelings about using drugs? What are the effects she gets from using drugs?

If your child has become a heavy user and would suffer severe physical withdrawl symptoms, especially when using alcohol, barbiturates, and/or narcotics, it's best to seek the immediate help of a drug rehabilitation program and medical expertise. If the addiction can possibly be handled without resorting to a drug program, use what you know about the child's drug use to work out an immediate emergency program—and plan this program *with your child*. Get her to make her own decision to stop using drugs. Also, help her avoid those people and/or circumstances which stimulate, encourage, or create the "right" mood for drug use.

Find out the real reason, not just the apparent reason, your child is taking drugs. While you are both handling the immediate drug situation, find out, through communication and observation, what seems to have brought about the drug use—is it a specific problem in school? Is she unable to deal with friends? Is her physical appearance bothering her? Does she have a fear of failure, or an actual failure? Is someone constantly belittling and invalidating her?

Avoid the temptation to evaluate; don't *assume* you know the real reason. Only your child knows the real reason, whether she's immediately aware of it or not.

One method to use in finding the reason for your child's drug use is to determine exactly when she first started using drugs, or *wanted* to use them. Then find out what happened or changed in her life at that time.

At this point, you must work to handle the problem or situation your child is trying to solve. The specific steps you take will depend on the nature of what is causing the drug use. There are some general principles to consider:

1. Help your child learn to handle the problem, that is, be able to take responsible action to whatever extent she can, even if only slightly at first. Then help her become more and more assertive as she gains confidence.
   For example, if she can't confront a whole group of children in the neighborhood, have her first confront one child who she feels most comfortable with. Then when that succeeds, involve her with two, and so on, until she feels confident enough to become involved with the entire group.
2. Avoid placing your child in situations or environments that tend to bring about use of drugs. (Could she live with a relative? Switch schools? Can you arrange things so that certain topics or actions or situations can be avoided?) Those types of things should be done in conjunction with a program to handle the cause of the drug problem.
3. Throughout the handling of your child's problem, help her develop her self-esteem and decision-making ability. Provide activities, projects, and situations which involve and motivate your child and in which she can succeed.

If you find you need assistance in handling the drug problem, look for a drug program whose goal is to improve your child's self-determinism. (In the reference section at the end of the chapter, sources are given that will help you find a drug rehabilitation program.)

THINGS TO DO

◆ *Complete the following basic checklist for helping develop your child's self-esteem.* (See also the checklist in Chapter One, which provides a specific list of things to do to help develop your child's self esteem.)

Checklist For Parents

	yes	no	sometimes
Do you help create opportunities in which your child will have success and accomplishment and develop her talents and abilities?			
Do you help ensure your child's success and accomplishment in what she does?			
Do you help your child become aware of, acknowledge, and validate her success and accomplishment, talents and abilities?			
Do you let others know of her successes, accomplishments, talents, and abilities?			
Do you let her demonstrate her capabilities to and for others?			

◆ *Complete the following checklist for helping your child learn to make decisions.*

Checklist For Parents

	yes	no	sometimes
Do you create or find opportunities in which your child can make a decision appropriate to her age, needs, situation, and capabilities?			
Do you help provide opportunities in which your child can evaluate, discuss, and learn from the decisions she makes?			
Do you allow your child the right to make a wrong decision?			
Do you provide alternatives from which your child can choose?			
Do you let your child experience the bumps, frustrations, and failures wrong decisions may bring about?			
Do you help your child become aware of the possible results and consequences of a decision she has to make?			
Do you hold your child responsible for the good and/or bad effects created by her decision?			

◆ *Reread the chapter and decide what topics best relate to your child.* List ideas as they come to you. Work out specific actions that will bring about desired changes. Discuss with your child what is to be done, and do it with her agreement.

◆ *Find out about the drug education program at your child's school.* Discuss with your child, her teacher, the school guidance counselor or the drug program coordinator. What are the aims of the program and the specific things that are being done? Is it an effective program?

◆ *Think about and discuss with your child any of the symptoms discussed on pp. 116–18 that may indicate her possible use of drugs.*

1. A change in routines and lifestyle
2. Important attitude and behavior changes
3. Sudden mood shifts
4. Paraphernalia of drug use
5. Generally more withdrawn and antisocial behavior
6. Physical changes and characteristics
7. General things not going well and getting worse
8. Frequent requests for money, or money and household items missing
9. A "gut" feeling that something is wrong with your child

SOME HELPFUL READING

Books

THE DRUG DILEMMA, by *Sidney Cohen, M.D.* (New York: McGraw-Hill Book Co., 1969). Dr. Cohen presents facts and viewpoints to better understand the drug problem.

THE CONSUMERS UNION REPORT ON LICIT AND ILLICIT DRUGS, by *Edward M. Brecher* and *The Editors of Consumer Reports* (Boston, Toronto: Little, Brown and Co., 1972). A comprehensive discussion, filled with information on drugs.

BEFORE ADDICTION: HOW TO HELP YOUTH, by *Florence Lieberman,* DSW; *Phyllis Caroff,* DSW; *Mary Gottesfeld,* MSW (New York: Behavioral Publications, 1973).

A SIGH OF RELIEF—THE FIRST-AID HANDBOOK FOR CHILDHOOD EMERGENCIES, produced by *Martin I. Green* (Toronto, New York, London: Bantam Books, 1977). This publication contains an excellent drug identification section, including pictures and descriptions of various drugs, their effects, treatment for overdoses or adverse reactions (pp. 70–72).

DECISIONS, DECISIONS, DECISIONS, by *Barbara Kay Polland* (photography by Craig DeRoy) (Millbrae, Calif.: Celestial Arts, 1976).

Organizations and Agencies (and How To Find Them)

To find drug rehabilitation organizations and agencies:

1. Use the phone book—look under Drugs, Narcotics, Alcohol; or find the listings for local, state, and federal government agencies and look under Drugs, Narcotics, Alcohol, Health Department, and Justice Department for references.
2. Ask the guidance counselor at your child's school for referrals and information.
3. Find your county, city, or state drug abuse coordinator, and ask that person for a directory or referral service.
4. *Narconon.* Narconon is a very effective national and international organization that is dedicated to the reduc-

tion of drug (and alcohol) abuse and crime, using the rehabilitation methods developed by L. Ron Hubbard. Narconon's approach is to help put responsibility back into the hands of the individual, and to allow the person to achieve his goals in life without drug or alcoholic dependence.

For information and literature, write: Narconon U.S., 6425 Hollywood Blvd., Suite 206, Hollywood, California 90028.

Pamphlets

Facts About ... This is a series of pamphlets that give basic facts about various drugs (tranquilizers, alcohol, barbiturates, tobacco, solvents and aerosols, amphetamines, PCP, opiates (narcotics), and hallucinogens). Information is given about the drugs, their specific short- and long-term effects, their toxic effects, the users, and reasons for their use.

For more information about these pamphlets, write:

Addiction Research Foundation of Ontario
33 Russell Street
Toronto, Ontario M5S 2S1

Catalogs

Narcotics Education, Inc. publishes a catalog that lists books, films, pamphlets, periodicals, posters, and teaching aids providing excellent information on drugs, alcohol, and tobacco. For the catalog, write to:

Narcotics Education, Inc.
P.O. Box 4390
6830 Laurel Street, N.W.
Washington, D.C. 20012

chapter 8

The Importance of Good Nutrition

BASIC VIEWPOINT

Children who are fed properly can increase their IQs and level of achievement in school.*

More and more people are becoming aware of the importance of proper eating. Medical doctors and educators are recognizing the importance of training people in the field of nutrition. Two major factors have contributed to this awakening: (1) illness can be prevented to a great degree when good nutrition is practiced, and (2) children who are properly fed can increase their IQ, level of achievement in school, and learning in general. It is the latter point that will be discussed in this chapter.

William T. Mullineaux, clinical director of the New York Institute for Child Development, and his associate, Dr. Alan C. Levin, did a study on a group of children who had previously been fed a "normal" supermarket-shelf diet consisting of excessive sugar, white-flour products, and foods containing chemical additives. For the study the children's

*Much of this chapter has been written by Donna Sanford, a parent who has devoted many years to studying and applying the principles of good nutrition.

diets were changed. They were fed a totally chemical-free natural diet consisting of a balanced amount from all the essential food groups. The results of the study showed a 20 percent increase in IQ over a period of one year!

This study shows that a proper eating program has a lot to do with your child's achievement in school—and hence with his success in life.

I SAW THE LIGHT

In Larry Groce's song "Junk Food Junkie" there's a lyric:

In the daytime I'm a natural
Just as healthy as I can be,
But at night I'm a junk food junkie
*Good Lord, have pity on me.**

The junk food addiction is very real to me. I've had my share of sweet and greasy food, but several years ago I Saw the Light!

Each year I'd try to get children I worked with to See the Light! I'd try everything. I used to have parties where the children had to choose sides. On one side of the room was the BD (body destroyer), "apologize-to-your-body" food; on the other side was the BB (body builder), "your-body-thanks-you" food. Once a child chose a side, it could not be changed.

The BD side would show off their white sugar candy bars, the BB side their brown- or non-sugar candy bars; the

---

*"Junk Food Junkie" by Larry Groce, published by Peaceable Kingdom, Los Angeles © 1976. All rights reserved.

BD side would hold up their chocolate cake, the BB side their organic carrot cake. The parties were fun.

I took classes to health food stores, had nutrition experts come to class, constantly brought in health food treats, explained about sugars and food additives. I'd tell them to read the ingredients on the package and (referring to the chemical additives) "if you can't read it, don't eat it!" Also, I was very careful never to be seen with my "rare imbibing" of a *scrumptious tasting* cream-filled cupcake.

In the following pages, written by Donna Sanford, you will receive a basic nutritional education—one that can be of tremendous help in the raising of your children, and more specifically, one that will show you how you can help your child do his very best in school.

THE PROPER EATING PROGRAM

Let's take a look at what is meant by a Proper Eating Program (PEP) and then at what you can do to establish a PEP with and for your children.

Why Is a PEP Important?

Sugar 'n spice 'n everything nice,
That's what little girls are made of.
Snakes 'n snails and puppy-dog tails,
That's what little boys are made of.

For as long as parents and their children have sung this little rhyme, little girls have been considered luckier than little boys. Actually, it's the little boys who were really the lucky ones. To understand why, it is necessary to look at how the human body responds to sugar.

What Happens to Food After It Enters the Body?

So that food can be used as fuel by the body, it must be chemically converted in the mouth and the stomach to a simple form of sugar called glucose. The body uses glucose to create warmth, cell nourishment, and energy. The pancreas, located behind the stomach, secretes a hormone called insulin which is the sugar-regulating hormone for the body. The adrenal glands, located in the lower back area, secrete a hormone called adrenalin, which contributes to a person's energy level. As long as natural, wholesome food is taken into the body, all these systems work harmoniously and evenly to keep the body's energy at a steady, smooth level.

What Occurs When Sugar Is Taken into the Body?

Taken directly into the mouth as a form of food, sugar does not have to go through all the stages of chemical conversion that normal, wholesome food requires. It is immediately absorbed into the bloodstream, and this causes the body to react as if it had received a shock. All systems go at an increased emergency level to handle the large and concentrated inflow of sugar.

The pancreas sends out a large amount of insulin (the sugar-regulating hormone) to handle all that sugar in the blood. This large amount of insulin then drives the blood-sugar level down so low that the individual desires *more* sweets (actually, sugar).

When more sugar is eaten, the body again acts at an

emergency level, causing that sudden "burst of energy" to occur. This is the reason most people believe that a candy bar or cookie is a good energy booster. However, the energy boost ends all too soon and is immediately followed by an overall letdown, during which the individual may feel dizzy, nauseous, very exhausted, or shaky. This overall letdown can cause difficulties in school, with concentration levels, learning rates, and attention span becoming less than optimum, and possibly leading to poor general health and well-being.

What Your Child Really Needs

What your child needs to maintain his energy level at a smooth, even pace is natural, wholesome food—food that allows the body to perform all of its activities as it is designed to do.

When natural protein like eggs, meat, and cheese and natural carbohydrates like vegetables, fruits, and grains are eaten, the body can smoothly and naturally go through its chemical conversions—starting in the mouth and continuing into the stomach, small intestine, and large intestine—systematically separating valuable food elements from bulk and waste, converting those elements into glucose. Through this continuous process a steady, even blood-sugar level is maintained, and this keeps the body operating smoothly.

The body is not built to handle a large and concentrated intake of sugar.

The White Bandit

For the purposes of explaining the importance of a Proper Eating Program to your child, we can rightfully call sugar "the White Bandit." Sugar robs the body of essential vitamins and minerals while traveling through it. The reason for this is that natural, whole foods that have not been processed and refined contain within themselves the vitamins and minerals needed to allow the body to digest them properly. White processed sugar has to rob the body of its own vitamins and minerals to be assimilated.

The Phantoms

The White Bandit has some company—let's call them "the Phantoms." These are the chemicals and preservatives used in processed, denatured foods, easily found on the supermarket shelf. Their name is a good one, because they are hidden and you can only identify them by their usually unpronounceable names, found in the ingredients listed on the food container. Dr. Ben Feingold* discovered that some of these White Phantoms—chemicals and preservatives in food—were a source of allergic reactions exhibited by many children. He placed hyperactive children on a high-protein, chemical- and sugar-free diet, and achieved great success. The children stopped being nervous and fidgety in class, were able to concentrate and spend more time on their schoolwork—and felt generally happier.

What to Include in Your Proper Eating Program

Here are the "Good Guys"—a list of food groups, with examples of natural and whole foods contained within each group:

*Ben F. Feingold, M.D., *Why Your Child Is Hyperactive* (New York: Random House, Inc., 1974).

Protein: nuts, meat, fish, cheese, beans, some vegetables, milk, eggs, whole grains, brewer's yeast, wheat germ, tofu (soybean curd), yogurt, kefir (cultured milk).

Carbohydrates: fruits, whole-grain breads, grains, macaroni products (made with whole grains, flours, soy flours, or seeds), beans, some vegetables with starch content, carob, natural sugars found in fruit, honey, molasses).

Fats and Oils: only cold-pressed oils and fresh butter. (Oils prepared by processing with extreme heat and chemicals are stripped of all vitamins and nutritional value.)

Vegetables and Fruits: all types of both these groups, preferably grown without chemical sprays and insecticides; if it is not possible to find chemical-free fruits and vegetables, there are effective methods for washing natural produce to remove any residuals that may be on the surface; whatever degree of these chemicals has grown into the plants during development cannot be eradicated.

The food in these groups comprises a basic list of foods to include in your PEP. There are numerous excellent books on nutrition available in bookstores and health-food stores that can help you increase your knowledge in this area. (See "Some Helpful Reading" at the end of the chapter.)

Some More Good Reasons for a PEP

People on a natural, wholesome diet—one that includes all the food groups— rarely need or desire drugs and excessive amounts of alcohol to compensate for the lack of energy and *joie de vivre* (joy of life) that's caused by nutritional deficiencies. When you provide a PEP for your child during his years of development, you are improving his chances to be free of these addicitons.

It has been observed that early nutritional deficiencies can lead to concentration problems, nervous habits, lack of good memory, sleeping troubles, and general laziness. These symptoms usually create emotional difficulties when they are not seen as possible signs of a basic nutritional problem.

When displayed, these symptoms are often "handled" by punishment, threats, and arguments causing conflict in the home and school. Certainly it is worthwhile establishing a PEP for your children, giving them the best possible chance of attaining success in school and in life.

Establishing a PEP is really not difficult at all, and your children will benefit many times over. They will know, especially as they grow older, that you cared enough to try just a bit harder. You will have the satisfaction of knowing that your extra effort has truly helped your children become better and happier individuals.

THINGS TO DO

◆ *Shopping and preparing for your PEP.* Go shopping with your children and play the game of "Supermarket Smarties." Have them identify the natural, wholesome foods, the Good Guys, and also the foods containing sugars and chemicals — the White Bandits and the Phantoms. Here are some to get you started:

The White Bandit & The Phantoms	The Good Guys
White bread	Whole-grain bread
Chocolate-drink mix	Cocoa (sweetened with honey)
Soda pop	Juices (unsweetened)
Sweet gelatin desserts	Plain gelatin, fresh-fruit gelatin
Cookies	Brown rice
White rice	Soya flour
White flour	Honey and molasses
Sugar	Whole-grain cereals
Sugared cereals	Unsalted nuts
Potato chips and pretzels	Sunflower seeds
Corn chips	Corn kernels with butter and sea salt
Rice mixes	Brown rice with herbs and vegetables

Let your children add items to each column of the list as they become more aware of the importance of a PEP. Each week, purchase one or two new types of fruits and vegetables. Introduce them to your children with enthusiasm. They will discover fruits and vegetables they especially like and will look forward to eating them often. As an added bonus, you will save money buying lots of fresh fruit and vegetables instead of prepared shelf items.

Natural-Food Cookbooks

Your local bookstore will have a selection of natural-food cookbooks which are sure to tempt your eyes and palate. I can promise you the discovery of a whole new (and healthy) world of delicious foods, from appetizers to desserts, that will furnish you and your family with unexpected adventures in eating. The kids can help you find "Good Guy" recipes that they can help prepare. Don't be surprised when your children volunteer to do the dishes, just to get a final lick at the batter bowl!

Preparation of Food

The way food is prepared is an important factor in the conservation or destruction of the natural vitamins and minerals found in food.

Steaming allows vegetables to soften and cook without being immersed in water, preventing the vitamins and minerals from being washed away. (Boiling causes the vitamins and minerals to be lost in the water.) Steaming also lets you get the full flavor of each vegetable, because the taste is not lost to the water. Steamers can be easily and cheaply purchased, if you don't already own one. You can find a stainless steel one that will fit in saucepans ranging from one quart to several quarts in size.

Baking vegetables with some fresh butter and just a small bit of water in a pyrex baking dish covered with some aluminum foil offers another tempting way to enjoy foods. Generally, the less your food is cooked, the more vitamins and minerals you will save. Try your meat a little less well done; don't soften your cooked vegetables as much.

Preparation of School Lunches

Pack nutritious and appealing lunches for your children. They will not only enjoy their food more, they will also reap the benefits of healthy food in the middle of the school day, enhancing their ability to learn and have a sense of well-being for the remainder of that day.

By purchasing or growing the foods listed earlier in the chapter, you will have all the tools necessary to prepare delicious, nutritious lunches. The following examples are suggested for quick and easy preparation. They are also convenient for your child to eat during a short lunch period.

Cream cheese, walnut, and sprout sandwich on whole-grain bread/Sliced Delicious apple/Thermos of carob milk. Spread cream cheese on lightly toasted whole-grain bread. Place a few walnuts in a plastic bag and grind them by pounding two or three times with a saucepan. Sprinkle walnut crumbs on cream cheese and top with a small handful of alfalfa sprouts.

Peanut butter 'n celery sandwich on whole-grain bread/ Large brown Bosc pear/Small box raisins/Thermos of milk. Dice a handful of celery and sprinkle it over whole-grain bread generously spread with crunchy peanut butter. (A variation on this is to substitute sliced banana instead of celery.)

Confetti cottage cheese and sprouts on whole-grain bread/ Carrot and celery sticks/Snakpak of raisins and sunflower seeds/ Thermos of peppermint tea with honey. Finely chop two small radishes, two scallions or ¼ small onion, and ¼ carrot. Mix into a small bowl of cottage cheese and sprinkle it with a natural all-purpose, vegetable-base seasoning. Spread on whole-grain bread (lightly toasted if you like). Top with alfalfa sprouts—and lick the bowl—it's delicious!

Avocado puree sprout sandwich/Chunk of cheese/Snakpak of dates/Thermos of herb tea flavored with fresh oranges. Peel avocado, mash in bowl. Add a natural all-purpose, vegetable-base seasoning, garlic powder, and dill weed (from the spice rack). Mix well. Spread on whole-grain bread. Top with sprouts. It's delicious—and quick!

For those children who come home for lunch, fixing food is really simple. As long as you're concentrating on keeping your family on a Proper Eating Program, they can have leftovers of chicken legs, fish or hamburgers, soups, yogurt, tofu pan-fried in butter with seasoning and a salad, or any of the above sandwiches as well as some healthy, taste-tempting delights that you dream up in your kitchen. Here are a couple of treat items that are good for luncheon desserts:

Frozen Bananas. Peel bananas, cut in half crosswise, place a stick through center, wrap in tin foil, and freeze. Give to the kids just like ice cream pops.

Orange Yogurt Bars. Squeeze six fresh oranges, remove pits from juice but leave any pulp that has passed through. Mix 2 ounces of plain yogurt with this and two to three tablespoons of honey. Place in popsicle holders, freeze, and then treat the kids to a tasty delight. (Vanilla yogurt will give you a sweeter popsicle.)

An additional note: suggesting some of these ideas at a PTA meeting could get a program started in your children's school to convert the cafeteria to a natural-foods program. Raisins and sunflower seeds in little paper cups, oatmeal cookies made with whole-grain flour, instead of cookies and cakes made with white flour and sugar (the Bad Guys), steamed or baked vegetables instead of French fries— wouldn't it be nice?

◆ *Checking Up on Yourself.*   Here's a checklist for you to complete to see if you are doing your best to maintain a PEP:

Checklist
_____

____ Did you plan your meals with PEP foods today?

____ Did you share the PEP experience with your children by making a game of it (such as the "Good Guy" foods vs. the "Bad Guy" foods)?

____ Did your children have "Good Guys" treats?

____ Did you see to it that your children had some fresh fruit?

____ If your children did eat more sugar then their bodies can handle, did you observe the effect it had on them? Did you explain it to them?

____ Did you observe the benefits your kids got from their PEP? Were they in a better mood? More enthusiastic? Less fidgety? More willing to listen to you? Have a better attention span? How was the color in their cheeks and the brightness in their eyes?

____ Did you allow your children to contribute to their PEP (select their own fruit or PEP cereal from the market)?

____ Did you check with their teacher(s) to find out how your children are doing in school since you've put them on a PEP?

A LAST NOTE

Where food is concerned,
Nature is best.
Give her a try,
She'll pass the test.

SOME HELPFUL READING

Mark Bricklin, The Encyclopedia of Natural Healing, Rodale Press, 1976.

William Dufty, Sugar Blues, Warner Books, 1975.

Ben Feingold, M.D., Why Your Child is Hyperactive, Random House, 1974.

Toni DeMarco, The California Way to Natural Beauty, Grosset & Dunlap, 1976.

E. Cheraskin, M.D., W.M. Ringsdorf, Jr., M.D., with *Arline Bricker,* Psychodietetics, Bantam Books, 1974.

Kurt W. Donsbach, Hypoglycemia, International Institute of Natural Health Sciences, 1976.

Frances Moore Lappé, Diet for a Small Planet, Ballantine Books, 1971.

Beatrice Trum Hunter, The Natural Foods Cookbook, Pyramid Publications, Inc., 1961.

Henry G. Bieler, M.D., Food is Your Best Medicine, Random House, 1965.

Adelle Davis, Let's Have Healthy Children, Harcourt Brace Jovanovich, Inc., 1951.

Gena Larson, BETTER FOOD FOR BETTER BABIES, Keats Publishing Co., 1972.

Sue Castle, THE COMPLETE GUIDE TO PREPARING BABY FOODS AT HOME, Doubleday and Co., Inc., 1971.

Benjamin Spock, M.D., BABY AND CHILD CARE, Pocketbooks, a division of Simon and Schuster, Inc., 1976.

Robert Rodale, ed. and publisher, PREVENTION MAGAZINE, Rodale Press.

Max M. Rosenberg, M.D., ENCYCLOPEDIA OF SELF-HELP, Books, Inc., 1950.

chapter 9

Health and Fitness

BASIC VIEWPOINT

Your child's health and well-being are important factors in her school experience; physical fitness has a great deal to do with success in studies.*

Have you ever tried studying when you had a 103-degree fever? a lower back pain? a severe headache? a case of diarrhea? It's not easy, is it?

When a child is attempting to study, attention should be focused on the necessary material and activities. However when a child is ill or not in top physical condition, there's a natural tendency to put attention on the body instead of on the materials and activities to be studied. An illness, poor physical condition, or a handicap can cause learning problems and hurt a child's chances for success in school.

For example, the American Optometric Association

*I am grateful for the contributions of Dan DiVito—an expert on physical fitness who has helped many adults and children become physically fit—for his assistance in the preparation of this chapter.

(AOA) reported in a newsletter how poor vision can contribute to students' learning difficulties, causing frustration, failure, and anger and often leading to nonproductive and antisocial behavior. One study reported that 80 percent of delinquent and semi-delinquent children had a learning difficulty, especially in reading, with poor vision being a contributing influence in 50 percent of those cases.

Be aware that the difficulty your child has in school (and in life) may possibly be caused by some unnoticed and/or untreated physical problem or disability.

AN UNFIT EXPERIENCE

This personal anecdote may remind you of similar experiences of your own.

Once when I was a sophomore in high school, I made the mistake of eating a lunch I knew would be trouble for me. Sure enough, while sitting in my social studies class I became aware of those body messages that said "OK, Bernard, your stomach is upset!"

I miserably waited for the class to end. I felt awful! I wasn't aware of anything that took place in the room. The social studies lesson had no interest or inspiration for me. All my attention was on my discomfort. For all I know the teacher may have called on me—if he did, I didn't hear him and couldn't have cared less. Educationally that was a wasted twenty minutes in my life.

In this chapter we will discuss some things to consider about your child's physical health and condition that could influence her school performance and attitude.

YOUR CHILD'S VISION

Your child's vision is an important factor in how well she succeeds in school, because so many activities depend on the use of sight. The American Optometric Association, in a pamphlet entitled, *Do You Know These Facts about Vision and School Achievement?* discusses four types of visual ability:

1. *Near vision*—The ability to focus and see clearly with both eyes and each eye separately at a distance of about 15 inches, the distance at which most desk work is done.
2. *Distant vision*—The ability to focus and see clearly with both eyes and each eye separately at a distance of 20 feet. This kind of vision is needed to see the chalkboard, movies, TV, and to take part in sports and other physical activities.
3. *Binocular vision*—The ability to make the two eyes work together. This is needed especially for efficient reading.
4. *Adequate field of vision*—The ability to see both sides, and up and down, while focusing on a small target without unnecessary eye-head movements. This ability is essential for sports participation and personal safety.

Your child's reading ability is obviously affected by her vision, and it goes without saying that many reading difficulties are caused by visual problems. For example: a child may not be able to see well close up; she may see separate unmerged images; letters or words may be reversed (for example, *tar* for *rat*); she may see only single letters or parts of words: eye movements may be slow; she may have astigmatism so that the print looks blurry; she may have trouble adjusting focus quickly when it is necessary to alternate from a short distance to a long distance and back (from a book to the board and back to the book).

There are many other types of vision difficulties and certainly other causes of reading failure, but be aware that a reading problem could be and often is caused or influenced by undetected vision problems.

Often vision problems are undetected, even by caring and responsible adults. One student of mine was unaware, as were her parents, that she had any vision trouble until she took one of the standard Sneller Eye Chart tests given in school (a very limited vision test). She had no trouble reading the chart with both eyes open, or with her left eye shut. But when she closed her right eye, she could see nothing. She was blind in her left eye, something neither she or her parents realized before that first school eye test.

A child's vision problems can cause frustration, confusion, upset, and difficulty in learning. Don't allow vision problems to act as a barrier to your child's growth and development in school and life.

What follows is a checklist prepared by the AOA to help indicate if your child is in need of a vision examination.

Checklist of Symptoms of Possible Vision Problems*

(As you read this list, note which items may relate to your child.)

General behavior

____ Clumsy—trips and falls over objects
____ Poor eye-hand coordination for age
____ Strains—thrusts head forward or squints eyes while looking at distant objects

*This checklist is based on material taken from pamphlets printed by the American Optometric Association, Inc.: *Check Your Child's Vision; Do You Know These Facts about Vision and School Achievement? A Teacher's Guide to Vision Problems.*

____ Poor performance on activity requiring visual concentration within arm's length (reading, coloring, writing, etc.)

____ Short attention span—unable to concentrate on visual tasks

____ Mainly takes part in outdoor activities (running, bicycling, etc.), avoiding activities needing visual concentration within arm's length

____ Tilting of head to one side or turning head to use only one eye

____ Placing head close to book or desk while reading

____ Frowning or scowling while reading, writing, or doing close work

____ Closing or covering one eye

____ Dislike for tasks requiring sustained visual concentration

____ Nervousness, irritability, restlessness, or unusual fatigue after maintaining visual concentration

____ Losing place while reading and using finger or marker to guide eyes and keep place while reading

____ Persistent letter reversals in reading, after the second grade (e.g., *b* for *d*, *tac* for *cat*)

____ Confusing similar words (e.g., *mile* for *mite*)

Appearance of eyes

(especially when visual concentration is needed)

____ Watering (tears in eyes)

____ Frequent blinking

____ Tendency to rub eyes

____ One eye turns in or out rather than looking directly at an object

____ Frequent sties or encrusted eyes

____ Eyes crossed or turning in, out, or moving independently of each other

____ Reddened eyes

Complaints associated with use of eyes

____ Headaches, nausea, dizziness
____ Burning or itching of eyes
____ Blurring of vision at any time

When Your Child Needs But Won't Wear Glasses

A common problem occurs when your child won't wear the glasses that will help her see better. There are many reasons for this. She may have the idea that wearing glasses is proof of some kind of personal weakness and failure; other children may tease her about the glasses ("Hey, four-eyes!").

You can help your child *want* to wear her glasses. Let her select the frame style she feels she looks good in (make sure they are durable enough to hold up under the rough treatment your child is bound to give them). Help her accept her glasses by finding examples of people she respects and looks up to who need and wear them. Show her how wearing glasses will help her see and perform better (see the board more clearly, do work more quickly, thus leaving time for other activities).

Make sure your child feels good when she uses her glasses.

YOUR CHILD'S HEARING

An inability to hear properly can be as detrimental to a child's education as poor vision. Children often develop attention and behavior problems as a result of hearing difficulties. It isn't uncommon to find that a child who is or appears to be disobedient, disruptive, a slow learner, or even retarded can't hear well.

I was once in a store with a child who had a severe hearing loss. The boy was looking at a toy he had taken off the shelf. The owner told him to put the toy back, but the child, because he was not wearing his hearing aid, didn't hear and so was unaware of what the owner was telling him. After two or three unsuccessful verbal attempts to get the hearing-impaired youngster to put the toy back, the owner became angry, snatched the toy away, and told him to get out of the store. Of course the child was confused and upset by the owner's obvious anger. After explaining the child's deafness to the store owner, he became most apologetic and felt very foolish.

I've also felt the embarrassment of analyzing a child's behavior as being disobedient, rude, or hostile only to find out that it was a hearing loss that had caused the lack of response I expected.

Children who, because of hearing loss, can't and don't properly follow directions or fully understand what is being said are bound to have difficulties in school.

What follows is a checklist that can help indicate if your child is in need of a hearing examination.

Checklist of Symptoms of Possible Hearing Problems

(As you read this list, note which items may relate to your child.)

  ____ Hearing head noises—hissing, ringing, whistling, roaring, booming sounds
  ____ Speech not properly developing at normal times (child may have a dull voice, with poor pronunciation, choice, and use of words)
  ____ Sudden loud noises do not startle child

_____ Frequent failure to hear words, phrases, and sounds that others hear (e.g., not hearing the phone ring when others do)

_____ Straining or thrusting one ear forward to hear

_____ Obvious loud noises or sounds seem normal or low to child

_____ Inattentiveness and failure to comply with verbal directions when child isn't looking at speaker (e.g., when child is in another room as you tell her something, or when back is turned, she doesn't respond)

As is true of vision problems, hearing trouble varies. It can be slight or great; the trouble may be with high- or low-pitched sounds; your child may be able to hear you, but not understand what you're saying; she may hear poorly at some times and almost normally at others.

Be attentive to your child's hearing ability—don't take it for granted. When children have unusual problems in school, whether academic or behavioral, a complete physical checkup may prove helpful in finding a cause. Don't overlook your child's hearing, especially if there's any indication of a possible hearing problem.

PHYSICAL HEALTH AND FITNESS

Is your child physically healthy and fit? That is, does she have a body that she doesn't have to put attention on because of any physical weakness, ailment, or problem? Does she have the vim, vigor, and vitality for carrying out the activities to be done throughout the day?

To be sure, being physically fit will not in and of itself

insure success at school. Yet, lack of physical fitness can certainly have a negative effect on your child's schooling.

Some of the areas to consider in helping maintain your child's physical health and fitness are dental care, physical checkups, rest and sleep, proper nutrition (see Chapter Eight), and exercise. In addition, as a parent you must watch for and deal with any symptom that indicates an illness or a physical problem.

In my experience of working with children, I've seen far too many instances in which poor physical health and fitness has interfered, to some degree, with performance in school. Not uncommon were children crying from the pain caused by cavity-ridden teeth, children falling asleep in class because of fatigue, children whose sole attention was on satisfying their sugar craving and as a result were not able to concentrate on their work, children generally too listless and starved for energy to take part in class activities.

How good your child feels, how strong she feels, and how much of a sense of well-being she has is very dependent on what kind of condition she keeps her body in. Activities that involve exercising have positive effects on the cardiovascular and respiratory system, help improve the digestive process, increase muscular development, strength, and endurance. These positive effects help the child sustain the physical and mental effort needed for school activities.

A body works best on motion, rather than inactivity. Bodies are built to be used, moved around, and exercised. If you just sit around, your body builds up wastes and toxins that are not beneficial and can lead to tiredness, sluggishness, and even sickness (all detrimental to achieving success in school and in life).

Your child should be involved in some form of physical exercise and activity. Help her find activities she enjoys and will participate in.

There are additional benefits of exercising. One is the feeling of success your child can have as she is doing and accomplishing something with her body. That feeling of being successful is a great energy booster that can carry over into other areas of life.

Another benefit is that the discipline and control of starting, continuing, and completing things, which exercise and fitness activities require, can carry over to other areas of life, including school and home. The sense of discipline (that is, the self-responsibility and control to learn and train at something with the intention of achieving a goal) can be invaluable in your child's school experience.

Your child should exercise often. Keep in mind the importance of gradual increases that will allow her to attain comfortable goals without causing muscular pain, soreness, and frustration. For example, it would be foolish to ask your child to ride a bicycle for 50 miles on the day she starts to ride.

Remember, the body works best on motion. There should be physical activity in your child's life—walking, jogging, jumping rope, playing volleyball, skating, bicycling, gymnastics, swimming, and so forth. These activities will improve her physical condition and maintain a state of good physical fitness and health.

The better condition your child's body is in, the more energetic she will be—able to sustain the effort, both physical and mental, that is needed for achieving success in school.

THINGS TO DO

◆ *Observe how physically healthy and fit your child is.*   Among the things you should keep an eye on are possible vision or hearing problems. (Use the checklists presented in the chapter.) Does your child have any recurring pains that are not related to any injury? Is your child excessively overweight or underweight? Does your child tire easily and often appear listless? Check your child's posture. Poor posture can cause fatigue and muscle strain. How is your child's overall appearance?

It is important for you to be aware of your child's physical health and fitness, and recognize that problems in school can be related to poor physical condition. Take your child for regular physical examinations and discuss with your child's doctor, chiropractor, or whoever helps protect your child's physical well-being what needs to be done to improve her physical condition.

◆ *Help your child learn about her body.*   The more your child knows and understands about her body, the more able she will be to take good care of it. This is a topic of great interest to most children. There are many books and other learning aids available (for example, models of the human body, pictures, skeletons) that can help give your child a better awareness of her body and how to care for it. (See the section at the end of the chapter for books that will help your child understand the human body.)

◆ *Help create a physical fitness program for and with your child.* Make this program real to your child through the presentation of information and discussion. Find activities your child enjoys that develop and work the body in various ways. It is best to include activities that build endurance, strength, flexibility, muscle tone, and balance. Select activities that are appropriate for your child's age and physical development. Be sure to establish a regular schedule for your child's exercise.

◆ *Get involved yourself.* If you are not already involved in a physical fitness program, get involved yourself and help motivate your child by setting an example. Find the program and/or activities that most interest and motivate you. Set a good example.

◆ *Find out what your child's school is doing for physical fitness.* All schools are required to have a physical fitness program. Find out what your child is doing to help condition her body at school. It should not be a token program, but should provide real benefit for your child.

SOME HELPFUL READING

Many books have been written on the care of the body and good health. Your library and local bookstore should have a selection of books on this topic.

For Children

HOW WE ARE BORN, HOW WE GROW, HOW OUR BODIES WORK . . . AND HOW WE LEARN, written and illustrated by *Joe Kaufman* (New York: Golden Press, 1975).

THE QUESTION AND ANSWER BOOK ABOUT THE HUMAN BODY, by *Ann McGovern,* illustrated by *Lorell M. Raboni* (New York: Random House, 1965).

For Adults

THE COMPLETE BOOK OF GOOD HEALTH—THE ILLUSTRATED FAMILY GUIDE TO DIET, FITNESS AND BEAUTY, edited by *Phoebe Phillips* and *Pamela Hatch* (New York: Thomas Y. Crowell Co., 1978).

FAMILY MEDICAL GUIDE, edited by *Donald G. Cooley* (New York: Better Homes & Gardens Books, 1973).

Fitness Activities and Programs

SUGGESTIONS FOR SCHOOL PROGRAMS—YOUTH PHYSICAL FITNESS, published by The President's Council on Physical Fitness and Sports, 1976. Available for $1.50 from:
The Superintendent of Documents
United States Government Printing Office,
Washington, D.C. 20402
(There is a minimum charge of $1.00 for each mailing.)

THE WEST POINT FITNESS AND DIET BOOK, by *Colonel James L. Anderson,* and *Martin Cohen* (New York: Avon Books, 1977). This book provides information on a conditioning program for all ages.

STREET GAMES, by *Alan Milberg* (New York: McGraw-Hill Book Co., 1976). This is a wonderful book filled with games and activities that will bring back memories to those of you who grew up playing street games. (Do you remember Ring-a-lievio?) You can have a lot of fun playing these games with your child.

Information on Deafness and Hearing Loss

Alexander Graham Bell Association for the Deaf
    3417 Volta Place N.W.
    Washington, D.C. 20007

National Association of Hearing & Speech Agencies (NAHSA)
    919 18th St., N.W.
    Washington, D.C. 20006

Information on Vision

The American Optometric Association
    7000 Chippewa St.
    St. Louis, Missouri 63119

chapter 10

Career Education

BASIC VIEWPOINT

Help your child become aware of and experience various career opportunities and learn what it means and takes to become a . . .*

"What would you like to be when you grow up?

How many times will your child hear that question? How often will he answer the question? How many times will his answer change?

One day a child might want to be a doctor, the next a teacher, then a rancher, or a chef. The reasons a child "decides" on a specific career are countless: his favorite movie star plays a doctor, or he knows that a rancher gets to ride a horse, or his physical education teacher is his current hero.

Basically, children decide on what they want to be when they become aware of and experience a career in some way (reading about it, seeing others do it, working at it) and find something about it that attracts them.

*Dianne Philips, a teacher and educator, and Virginia Fair, a business and management consultant, both of whom are concerned with career education, helped prepare this chapter.

Parents have the responsibility to ensure that their children are made aware of and experience various career opportunities, whether they provide these experiences themselves or help ensure that their children's school has a meaningful career education program (especially at the high school level). It's then up to children to decide for themselves, based on the information and viewpoints they have received, what career direction they would like to head in.

If parents can help their children handle the uncertainty they feel about future careers, they've helped them towards happier lives.

THE SIGH OF RELIEF

When I was 9-years-old, I remember standing in a subway station and looking at a couple of men sweeping garbage from between the tracks. I thought to myself, "Who will do this kind of work, or be a garbage man, or shoemaker, in the future?" I "knew" everybody would be a doctor, teacher, businessman, or lawyer, and there would be no one to do the other jobs.

I "knew" this because my father, a butcher, and my mother, who sewed seat covers for upholstery companies, helped instill attitudes towards various occupations by what they valued, exposed me to, and expected of me.

When I started college I knew all the things I *didn't* want for a career, but I didn't know exactly what I wanted to do. I did what many students did when they were uncertain of their future: I majored in psychology. I hoped to "find myself" while learning what you learn when studying psychology.

Happily, I found my real area of interest, concern, and ability in my junior year—teaching and education. It was with a big sigh of relief and a bit of trepidation that I decided to major in education. The trepidation was based on the fact that out of a group of 350 students majoring in education, 348 were women. (I must admit that I found the experience most enjoyable.) The sigh of relief was because I had found what I wanted to study, to be what I wanted, to do what I wanted, to have what I wanted.

How do people decide what they want to do? How can parents help their children decide on a fulfilling and rewarding career?

In this chapter we will discuss what you as parents can do, and/or urge your child's school to do, to help your child become aware of the career direction he will take.

The proper school placement and program of learning (especially from high school on up) will depend on how successfully your child has identified the career direction and opportunities he should take advantage of.

STEPS IN CAREER GUIDANCE

*The Dictionary of Occupational Titles** lists over 20,000 occupations; these have been broken into fifteen career groupings by the Office of Education:

Agricultural Business and Natural Resources
Business and Office
Communication and Media

The Dictionary of Occupational Titles, 4th ed., 1977. Published by the U.S. Department of Labor, U.S. Employment Service.

Construction
Consumer and Homemaking
Environment
Fine Arts and Humanities
Health
Hospitality and Recreation
Manufacturing
Marine Science
Marketing and Distribution
Personal Service
Public Service
Transportation

Career exposure and experiences can and should start as early as possible. The years from birth through age 6 are known to be an exceptionally important time for developing a child's attitudes, viewpoints, and abilities.

Discuss with your child careers related to the people and things you see as you're walking, shopping, or visiting; recommend and/or read books that relate to careers; have your child see certain films or TV shows that help him learn about or interest him in different careers. The opportunities are limitless.

Obviously it's impossible for your child to be exposed to every possible career. You will have to use opportunities as they naturally come up, as well as deliberately planning for meaningful experiences with particular careers.

Utilize Friends, Family, and Acquaintances as Sources of Information and Career-related Experiences

When I was growing up my father would take me to his butcher shop; my friend took me to Ebbets Field (where the Brooklyn Dodgers played), and I met his uncle who was the head groundskeeper there. I went to my cousin's factory. I was given many experiences that helped me determine what I *didn't* want to do and led me to what I decided upon for a career.

Think about the various careers of the people you have any connection with, and you'll find an abundance of potential career-related experiences for your child.

Utilize the Specific Interests, Abilities, and Talents of Your Child

In observing your child, look for areas of interest, special abilities, and talents; utilize whatever resources you can to help your child experience the potential for developing a career around those interests, abilities, and talents.

Helping your child experience different career opportunities should be a natural, easy part of growing up. Children are eager to learn and involve themselves in those things that are of interest to them, and in which they have ability and talent to successfully work and create.

Help Your Child's Dreams Become Reality

It is important for parents to help their children create and nurture their dreams and goals, and at the same time prepare them for the practical realities of life. This can be one of the most difficult roles of parents.

How many of your dreams and goals have been taken away because of the practical realities you've had to face? How many times have you had to compromise, or do things you didn't really want to do? Have *you* stopped dreaming or trying to fulfill your dreams?

Help your child find and keep dreams that can become reality. Find good role models for him to look up to, people

who've succeeded at bringing their dreams to reality, no matter what their background and upbringing. In doing this, help your child take into consideration his skills, interests, and talents. Expose him to dream creating experiences through trips, shows, meeting people, books, and so on.

Help him learn to combine his dreams with the practical realities of survival.

A PROGRAM FOR HELPING YOUR CHILD FIND A CAREER DIRECTION

What follows is a suggested program to help your child choose a career direction. It's intended to help young people decide such questions as whether or not to continue on in school, what school to attend, what courses to take, and so forth.

List with your child everything he considers important in a job. Such things as money, location, environment, work hours, co-workers, and so forth should be considered. Also, discuss and list (even have him demonstrate) the type of lifestyle your child would like to have (family, or single; city, country, or suburban living; and so forth).

Help your child discover his strong points. What are his special skills and talents? What things does he work at and create most easily that give him the most enjoyment? What is he most interested in having, doing, and being?

Find out what may have interested him in the past but no longer does. Let your child communicate his feelings and thoughts about why he lost interest, and find out whether he would like to rekindle it. You can help by knowing that two major reasons for loss of interest in a subject or activity are *improper study methods* and *lack of success in producing the products of that subject or activity.* Use the information from Chapter Four to help your child handle anything he may have misunderstood about the subject, and help ensure that he has successful and meaningful experiences related to it.

Find and use books that list occupations (OCCUPATIONAL OUTLINE HANDBOOK *and* DICTIONARY OF OCCUPATIONAL TITLES *are two good ones).* Have your child write down the areas that seem to align with his interests, skills, talents, and preferences for an ideal job and lifestyle.

Many career books tell what training is involved in various fields, as well as where the training can be obtained, the costs involved, and a brief description of a typical day in the life of a person within that career.

Help your child learn the practical realities of the fields that interest him. Consult with local universities, high schools, vocational training schools, training centers, private companies and corporations, or individuals involved in the field of interest. Ask for pamphlets, request to sit in on a class or observe a day or week in the actual work environment.

Utilize your child's school. Promote the idea, with the school principal and parents' committees, of actively seeking to use parental and community resources to help students learn more about different careers. For example, a list could be made of the various occupations of parents whose children attend the school. These parents could be called on to lecture and/or take part in an educational program related to their career. Through parents and community businesses, opportunities can be created for young people to learn about careers and even apprentice where possible.

Have your child work on projects related to a career choice. If he wants to be a mechanic, find the opportunities in which he can work on mechanical objects; if he is interested in the medical profession, he might help care for a sick member of the family, or get a part-time job (or volunteer position) in a hospital.

Narrow down the choices. Look over the practical realities of the possible careers. What are the educational requirements? The cost of education in the field? How qualified is your child based on his education and background? Where can the career education be acquired? How long will it take? How obtainable is a job in that career? Where would your child have to work and live? What is the likely income from such an occupation? What hazards are involved, if any?

To further narrow down the choice, have him decide

which occupation best matches up to his personal ideal situation in life.

When he has decided on a career direction, ask what he would like to gain from his career choice; list the rewards.

Discuss and find out what things could *stop* your child from being able to have his desired career. Find out what has to be done to handle these barriers. Help him obtain information, utilize resources, get the appropriate training, and do whatever is necessary to overcome any possible barriers.

Be willing for your child to make his own decisions. Your role as a parent is to guide, motivate, help out in whatever way possible, but you must recognize that the ultimate decision your child makes is his own. To try to force a child to conform to *your* wishes is to promote failure.

THINGS TO DO

The activities to follow should be undertaken when they fit naturally into your child's needs while growing up. Don't force or demand that your child do these things. They will be beneficial only when he agrees with your program.

◆ *Make a list of your child's interests, skills, and talents.*   The list can be based on your own observations and discussions with your child and people who know him (teacher, friends).

◆ *Make a list of potential family, friends, and acquaintances who could be resources and provide career-related experiences.*   Work out an arrangement with other people to help provide and share resources, information, and experiences that relate to career awareness development.

♦ *List other possible resources that relate to your child's skills, interests, and talents.*

♦ *Find out about the career education program in your child's school.* Find out how you can use it, or if need be, work to improve it.

♦ *Find and provide appropriate training and preparation.* Help your child develop skills, talents, and interests in possible career directions (dancing lessons, apprenticeships, and so forth).

SOME HELPFUL READING

DICTIONARY OF OCCUPATIONAL TITLES (U.S. Department of Labor).

OCCUPATIONAL OUTLOOK HANDBOOK (U.S. Department of Labor).

LOVEJOY'S CAREER AND VOCATIONAL SCHOOL GUIDE, by *Clarence E. Lovejoy* (New York: Simon & Schuster, 1978).

chapter 11

Your Rights as a Parent

BASIC VIEWPOINT

With a working knowledge of what you as a parent have a right to expect the schools to provide you and your child, you can have a greater control of the quality of education that child receives.

Schools are constantly making decisions and taking actions that will affect your child's schooling. These relate to such matters as what her class placement should be; what special programming she may or may not need; what special courses of instruction will be taught to your child's class; what is written and placed in your child's record cards; who has the right to have access to your child's record cards; who shall teach your child's class; and how your child will be disciplined.

When situations arise that you're not pleased with, or question, you should know what you can do and where you can go to help handle what is happening.

The key words of this chapter are *find out*!

Find out what your legal rights and limitations are and what you can and can't do for yourself and your child. Find out how you can work for change when you believe change is needed.

YOU'RE IN TROUBLE

The third year I was teaching I got one of those "you're in trouble with the principal" messages. I was told to get down to his office *immediately*. I was surprised—I wasn't aware I'd done anything wrong and wondered what had caused his anger.

When I got to his office he handed me completed application forms for special school placement that had been filled out and returned by the parents of some of my students. He asked, "Why did you give these out before you were supposed to?"

I explained that I had only given the forms to the parents who had formed a committee and actively pressured the school authorities to create the limited openings in these special schools. I felt it was their right to have the first chance at putting their children in one of the schools if they wanted to do this, because it was their efforts that had provided the opportunity.

Since the way children were to be chosen and placed in the schools depended on who was first to hand in an application, I felt it would be unfair to the parents on the committee if their children were not selected.

The principal explained that there were legal rights that had to be considered, and though my action seemed ethically right, it violated the rights of other parents and children. When the decision to send children to special schools was approved by the school system, this meant that *all* the parents had the right to apply in behalf of their children.

When I explained the principal's position to the parents on the committee, they were most upset and felt their rights had been ignored, and they protested vehemently.

As it turned out, all of the committee's children eventually were selected for placement in the schools.

This chapter will provide some basic information on the education-related legal rights of parents. At the end of the chapter is a listing of sources that will give a more complete treatment of the topic.

CHILDREN'S AND PARENTS' EDUCATIONAL RIGHTS

Know and understand that you as a parent have rights in regard to your child's schooling. To quote from *The Rights of Parents in the Education of Their Children*, "The rights are of two kinds . . . the rights parents have on their own as parents and the right they have as agents for their children . . ."

In brief, the rights you and your children have as related to education are the following:*

The right to a free education.
The right to be protected against harm.
The right to inspect student records.
The right to special education for students with special needs.
The right to due process of law.
The right to equal educational opportunity.
The right to freedom from unreasonable search and seizure.
The right to freedom of expression.
The right to freedom of religion and conscience.

Your legal rights (and limitations) regarding the schooling of your child may vary depending on the state in which you live. Rights such as those dealing with your child's

---

*The Rights of Parents in the Education of Their Children, by David Schimmel and Louis Fischer (Columbia, Maryland: The National Committee for Citizens in Education, 1977), p.1.

instruction, school disciplinary procedures, and records are established from these main sources: the federal and state constitutions; the legal tradition called the common law as it is reflected in the decisions of the courts; laws and regulations of the federal and state governments; and local school board policies.

How do public school systems work? The following list should help you understand:

1. The U.S. Constitution puts states in charge of education.
2. State legislatures generally make statements about educational goals and programs.
3. State legislatures give the boards of education and local district boards the responsibility to carry out these programs.
4. The local board usually has the main authority and responsibility for hiring and firing teachers and administrators; establishing priorities; choosing textbooks; and resolving educational disputes among competing groups of parents, teachers, administrators, and students.

5. The local board selects a school superintendent who administers the local board policies to the schools in the district.
6. The local boards are elected and responsible to the community for its goals and programs.
7. The school principal follows the policies of the school board as administered by the superintendent.

HOW TO PROTECT YOUR CHILDREN'S EDUCATIONAL RIGHTS

How can you protect your children's (and your) educational rights? Here are some guidelines:

☐ Demand that the principal or school officials at your local district office provide you a written list of your legal rights in the state and community in which you live, regarding a specific issue you're concerned with.

☐ Decide who would best handle the area of concern. (Is it the teacher, assistant principal, principal, district superintendent, local school board members?) If you're not sure who to go to, ask the school principal, or call your local school district office.

☐ Work for changes if you believe they are necessary. To do this, you can write your legislator; try and influence the locally elected board; organize support by getting petitions signed; get people to attend meetings. (You should use concrete specific facts, not just opinion and rumor, to support your position.)

☐ Find out how best to work with the people who hold the power in the schools.

☐ Use the sources listed at the end of the chapter.

You can make a change by using your legal rights. Every day meaningful changes are being made by parents who know and use their legal rights. For example, in my school a group of very vocal, strongly intentioned parents worked to get a man of their choosing to become principal of the school. They struggled and had to overcome much opposition, but got *their* principal.

A friend of mine had a child in a class where the teacher was indifferent and ineffective (to say the least). The parents of the children in that class decided to do something about it, and they were able to always have one parent in the room observing the class. The purpose was to help the teacher take more responsibility for what occurred in the classroom. Eventually, the teacher left the school.

Know your rights, demand your rights, and you'll be better able to help make your child's school experience a positive and constructive one.

THINGS TO DO

◆ *Find out about your and your children's educational rights.* You can get a Parents' Rights Card and a lot of helpful information by writing the National Committee for Citizens in Education (NCCE), (410 Wilde Lake Village Green, Columbia, Maryland 21044—Dial toll free 800–638–9675). The NCCE provides information that helps parents share in school decisions affecting their children.

◆ *Observe your child's schooling, and list any questions you have about his rights or yours being violated.* Discuss these with the appropriate person.

◆ *Demand to see* in writing *the law and/or policy that's being used when you feel your or your child's rights are being violated.*

SOME HELPFUL READING

THE RIGHTS OF PARENTS IN THE EDUCATION OF THEIR CHILDREN, by *David Schimmel* and *Louis Fischer*(Columbia, Maryland: The National Committee for Citizens in Education, 1977).

THE RIGHTS OF STUDENTS, by *Alan Levine*, with *Eve Cary* and *Diane Divoky* (available for $1.50 from The American Civil Liberties Union, 221 East 40th Street, New York, N.Y. 10016).

chapter 12

Television:
Use It,
Don't Abuse It

BASIC VIEWPOINT

Television is a tool that can be used positively. Avoid abusing it, or allowing it to abuse you and/or your child.

Much has been said and written, both pro and con, about the effects of TV on children. There can be no doubt of its influence; children tend to spend more time watching TV than doing any other activity (except sleeping). It has been estimated that by the time the average child graduates from high school he will have watched 15,000 hours of TV, and will have spent 12,000 hours in school.*

There are basically two things to consider when we discuss the influence of TV: the effect the content of TV shows has on your child, and the effect that persistent TV watching has on your child (which I believe has more importance than the content of shows).

Some of the commonly heard arguments against TV are that it makes children passive (less self-motivated and active);

* Raymond Coppola, "What if Wonder Woman Teamed Up with the Hulk?" *TV Guide*, December 30, 1978, pp. 24–26.

that it stifles children's imagination; that it brings about a shortened attention span; that it interferes with a child's socialization and ability to deal with and relate to real people; that it keeps children from doing other things they could be doing; that it imparts values that parents may not be in agreement with; that it has a negative effect on the development of verbal abilities (including reading, writing, and speaking); that it lessens to a marked degree the importance of real-life experiences, and encourages a tendency to think about things based only on viewpoints seen on TV; and that it dilutes the quality of family life and relationships.

Some of the positive claims are that it helps build the vocabulary of young children; that it can stimulate interests and motivate actions; that it can provide fine entertainment; that it can inform children in a unique and important way; and that it can help children develop positive attitudes, values, and comprehension.

There's no doubt that TV will affect your child's survival. It's up to you, the parent, to observe and understand the impact it has, and to develop the awareness and control to ensure that TV is used as a positive tool by and for your child.

CHARLES MEETS THE FONZ

When I began teaching in the 60s, Black Power and militancy were becoming quite assertive. I was teaching in a school in which 98 percent of the students were black, and I had to deal with the personal anger, pride, and other assorted attitudes of my students and the school community toward white people. In the late 60s and early 70s, if any of my students outwardly expressed their liking for a white over a black performer, athlete, or any contemporary newsworthy individual, they would be met with hostility, disagreement and dismay by near unanimous response.

I'd gotten used to that viewpoint and in many ways felt it a good and healthy thing. Then one day in 1975 I noticed something about Charles, the toughest, black, street-oriented kid in my class. He was wearing a shirt with a picture of The Fonz (a *white*, male, street-wise character on the TV show, *Happy Days*). Charles was walking around the room imitating The Fonz's style of "cool."

It turned out that The Fonz was the personality many of the children in class most wanted to emulate—a white personality. This change in attitude had been brought about through TV. At that moment I realized more than ever what an important influence TV is on the lives of children.

One of the most important judgments to be made by parents concerns when to allow a child freedom of choice in what he does and when to put up the "stop sign" that definitely, and with consistency, places limits on what a child can have, do, and be. TV is one area in which it is necessary to know when to put up the "stop sign."

In this chapter you will find ideas to help you better judge how you can control the use of TV and avoid letting it become a nonconstructive, or even harmful, influence on your child.

THE VALUE AND PURPOSE OF TV

Before deciding how to best use TV, you should decide on what its value and purpose is in relation to your child's needs. This will help you decide how and when to limit your child's viewing (whether it be an absolute or partial ban, or unlimited freedom of choice).

Find out about the certain and probable effects TV viewing will have on your child. In her book *The Plug-In Drug,** Marie Winn makes a very strong case for severely limiting, if not totally eliminating, your child's television viewing. She believes that TV is seriously implicated as a contributing factor in the declining verbal abilities of children; in trends such as drug use and abuse; in a changing lifestyle leading to less meaningful interaction between children and their families. She also believes TV leads to passivity, having generally negative effects on the way children think and behave.

Reading books and articles presenting various opinions about TV is one good way to get information. You can also discuss TV's effects with other parents, friends, teachers, and so on. List the basic values and attitudes you would like to impart to your child, and determine how TV would contribute to or detract from these. Observe the actual effects TV has on your child, especially in regard to those values and attitudes you would like to impart.

Only when you have developed certainty concerning the purpose and value of TV in your child's life can you best decide on how to control and limit TV viewing.

Be Firm and Consistent in Your Decisions

The firmness, consistency, and decisiveness of any decision you make will depend on your certainty as to the value and purpose of TV.

Recognize that your child will probably have strong reasons to resist any limitations on his TV viewing (especially if no real control has ever been established). For instance,

* New York: The Viking Press, 1977.

there are shows your child genuinely enjoys and is interested in watching. He may have developed a TV habit that will be hard to break. There will be reasons personal to each child's needs and wants that can best be defined by observation and discussion with him. Your own viewing habits, if they are excessive, may cause him to question your actions to limit his viewing. Also, peer pressure will exert its influence: "My friends will think I'm strange," "My friends all watch," "I'll be left out of what's happening, and they'll all know about it."

I remember several years ago I had no TV. When my class asked me about my favorite TV show and I told them that I didn't have one, they found it hard to believe. When I finally convinced them that I didn't own one, they gave me one of those "you sure are strange, how could you live without it" looks. I almost felt I had better go out and buy one or else my class would never trust me again.

When making your decision about how to control and limit TV viewing, it is best to get your child's understanding and agreement; but even if you can't, you have to enforce the decision based on your certainty of what the greatest good will be for your child.

HOW TO CONTROL THE USE OF TV

As you read the following suggestions, use them as springboards to developing a method that will work best for you and your child. You might select a couple of alternatives and let your child choose which one he most agrees with; or you could allow your child to help devise his own schedule for watching. These are very practical ways of getting his cooperation.

Here are some suggestions for controlling your child's TV viewing:

Only allow a certain number of shows or hours of viewing per day and/or week.

Don't allow viewing until certain responsibilities, assignments, or activities are completed—for example, homework, room cleaning, dinner.

Allow unlimited viewing of certain types of shows, limited viewing of others.

Don't allow TV during the school week.

Discuss with your child your negative feelings about TV viewing in general (or specifically, regarding certain shows); your viewpoints, expressed to your child, can have a strong impact on when and what he will watch.

Sharply limit your own TV viewing (if needed).

Ban all TV viewing.

Only view TV for very special shows (no viewing on any regular basis).

Use the various TV listings to decide with your child what shows can be seen according to whatever limits are decided on.

Help arrange and develop a rich and active social, creative, and productive lifestyle for your child, in which TV viewing becomes less necessary and wanted.

Make the act of TV watching less than pleasant and easily accessible. You can keep an old and/or poorly functioning set that would only be watched when there's a *real* need or desire; or insist on the TV being stored in a closet, or out-of-the-way place when not being viewed; or keep the TV in an unpleasant viewing environment (an unfurnished basement); or place it in a part of the house where it's not too convenient, or easily gotten to.

HOW TO USE TV

When you read the following ideas on ways to use TV as a meaningful learning tool, please understand that *your* judgment will determine what is relevant to the needs and interests of your child.

Helping Your Child to Be an Active TV Viewer

The more creative and productive your child is, the happier, more active, and more successful he will be. Yet watching television gears children to be uncreative and unproductive. Find ways to actively involve your child in what he's watching, in some creative and productive manner. Here are some suggestions you might be able to use:

Act along with the show (pantomime one of the characters, pretend to be the star of the movie, etc.).

Have your child observe specific things in a show (the types of cars, style of dress, different accents). The type of show will dictate the kinds of things to look for.

Sketch a character, car, home, anything that will be seen more than once during the show.

Listen for new vocabulary; for fact and opinion statements (especially in commercials and the news), etc.

Have your child move around and do some type of exercise if he's watching a show that lasts over a half-hour (e.g., stretching, twisting).

Discuss the Shows Watched

The opportunities and need for discussion will vary according to the nature of the show watched and the needs and interests of the child who is watching. Among the things you might discuss are why he wants to watch a show. Did he get what was hoped for from watching a particular program? Elicit specific questions, problems, issues, feelings, ideas, or information that relate to the program. Find out what he liked or disliked about the show. Ask him how he thinks the ideas a show presents can be used in his life. How would he have done the show differently? Does he believe the commercial? These are only a few discussion topics that will make TV viewing more constructive.

Develop Writing Skills

After viewing a show, you can have your child write a brief description of the show, like those that are written in a TV guide. (A comparison could be made between the child's description and one in an actual TV guide.) Another idea is to have him write fan letters to stars, or write opinions of the program and send them to the producer with suggested changes and/or additions. Or he could take notes from a program, especially one presenting ideas and viewpoints on a topic of interest to him. How about asking him to write a script based on the characters of a TV show? Or even write script ideas and send them to the producer.

Use and Develop Reading Skills

Have your child read descriptions of the shows on TV, especially to decide what shows to watch. Have him read articles about favorite shows and stars. He could also use written materials prepared specifically for some shows, such as those that have their scripts published so that children can read and follow the script as the program is on. (Your child's school would receive information about when these special shows are aired.) Another exercise is to have him read the credits after the show. For example, ask the child to find the director's name, the producer's last name, and so forth. Be sure your child understands the words found in the credits.

Prepare Your Child to Watch Certain Shows

Where appropriate, select shows you would like your child to watch and prepare him with information, ideas, and relevant material that will make the show more meaningful. Docudramas, documentaries, historical films, special plays, and movies readily lend themselves to this idea.

Vary the Content of the Programs

Help your children select a balanced pattern of programs—he shouldn't watch only cartoons, comedy, adventure, and sports, but also documentaries on topics of interest, drama, historical movies, and so forth.

Plan Follow-Up Activities and Materials

Those programs that spark a child's interest in becoming more involved in some subject matter should without a doubt be followed up. Some activities could include books to read; trips, where possible and appropriate; craft activities; discussion of the show.

Be Ready to Handle the Effects a TV Show May Have on Your Child

Observe your child during and after he watches shows. See what type of effects the show(s) have (good, bad, indifferent), and decide how to deal with those effects. For example, reinforce the good effects through appropriate activities; handle bad effects by discussing the problem created by the show and possibly stopping your child from watching the show.

Evaluate the Value and Purpose of Specific TV Shows

Make a list of the values, attitudes, and beliefs you feel your children should acquire (such as respect for others and their property, working together to accomplish goals, not lying or cheating to get ahead). When you evaluate programs,

TV Viewing Chart

Who	What	When	Where	Why	Follow-up
John	*Mash*	Mon., 9:30P.M.	Own room	Entertainment	None
Mary John	*That's Cat*	Sun., 6:00P.M.	Mary's room	Fun; to observe new things; to develop new interests.	Sketch one thing you really liked; find book on a topic that interested you.
Mary	*After-School Special*	Thurs., 4:00P.M.	Own room	Entertainment; develop understanding of the show's theme.	Discuss with parents.

compare the values, attitudes, and beliefs they present with your own list.

The Committee on Children's Television (see resource section at end of chapter) has presented certain standards for evaluating TV programs. These standards include such questions as whether or not the program motivates constructive activities, encourages worthwhile ideas, values, and beliefs, and so forth.

Care of the Eyes

The American Optometric Association, in its pamphlet *To View Or Not to View,* makes recommendations on the best way to watch TV. Here are some of this group's recommendations:

There should be a distance between the child and the TV set of at least five times the width of the picture.

TV shouldn't be watched in a completely dark room; soft overall lighting should be used.

Avoid placing the TV set where there will be glare or reflections from lights or windows.

Have the TV set at eye level; avoid looking up or down at the picture.

Rest occasionally by briefly looking away from the picture.

THINGS TO DO

◆ *Reread the chapter and decide what things best relate to you and your child.*   List ideas as they come to you. Work out specific actions that will bring about desired changes and improvements. Discuss with your child what's to be done.

◆ *List the values, attitudes, and beliefs that are important to you as parents.*   Discuss the best ways you can use TV to implement these values.

◆ *Discuss and list why you allow your child to watch TV* (as a babysitter; it pacifies; it is too hard to battle over with your child; to be entertained; and so on).

◆ *Establish agreements with your child about the use and control of TV.*   He will be more cooperative if he understands your reasons and helps decide.

◆ *Decide the when, where, what, why, and who, of TV use in your home.*   A chart similar to the one presented here can be developed.

◆ *Work out with your child's teacher ways to use TV as a learning tool.*   There are many ways to implement the school's curriculum with TV viewing. Discuss with the teacher (and perhaps the PTA, and the school principal) how to best utilize TV with the program of instruction your child is receiving.

♦ *If your child views TV excessively, find out the reasons for this and deal with the problem*   There can be many reasons for excessive TV watching—but don't *assume* that you know what they are. Discuss with your child his feelings; observe what he may be lacking in his life (a meaningful hobby that interests him, friends to play with, too little responsibility). Work out the best way to handle the problem.

SOME HELPFUL READING

Books

THE PLUG-IN DRUG, by *Marie Winn* (New York: The Viking Press, 1977).

THE FAMILY GUIDE TO CHILDREN'S TELEVISION, by *Evelyn Kaye* (New York: Pantheon Books, 1974).

TELEVISION'S CHILD, by *Norman S. Morris* (Boston and Toronto: Little, Brown and Co., 1971).

REMOTE CONTROL, by *Frank Mankiewicz* and *Joel Swerdlow* (New York: Time Books, 1978).

Organizations

Action For Children's Television is a nationwide, action-oriented consumer organization involved in improving the quality of TV for children. This group has material that will help you better understand what you can do to improve the quality of your children's TV experience. For information, write:

Action For Children's Television(ACT)
46 Austin Street
Newtonville, Massachusetts 02160

Committee On Children's Television is an organization composed of a diverse group of people concerned with improving children's TV. Like ACT, this group can provide assistance and materials that will help with your child's TV viewing. For information, write:

Committee On Children's Television (CCT)
1511 Masonic Avenue
San Francisco, California 94117

National Citizen's Committee for Broadcasting
1346 Connecticut Avenue, N.W.
Washington, D.C. 20036

Federal Communication Commission (charged with regulating the broadcasting industry)
1919 M Street, N.W.
Washington, D.C. 20036

The American Optometric Association will send a free pamphlet concerning eye care and TV viewing, entitled *To View or Not to View.* Write:

American Optometric Association
7000 Chippewa Street
St. Louis, Missouri 63119

chapter 13

The Junior High School Years— A Time of Change

BASIC VIEWPOINT

The junior high school years are ones in which young people are trying to establish their identities—their own viewpoints. This is a time of change, new awarenesses, and new possibilities. These years can be a time of joy, excitement, and opening up. They can also be a time of doubts, fears, and frustrations. It is essential that children be given the freedom to explore the new possibilities these years open up for them; at the same time they must be given realistic boundaries through the guidance, communication, and good control provided by you, the parent.*

*I believe it is important to discuss the junior high years in a separate chapter. These years can be and often are a very difficult time for children and, naturally, for their parents. Issues concerning such things as peer pressure, sex education, and communication are very real ones that influence a child's school experience and carry over into the high school years and adult life.

Though the material of this chapter is geared to the junior high years, much of the data is applicable to all ages, especially the section on communication.

This chapter was mainly written by Davina Rubin, who has worked with, studied, and been extensively involved with children in the "perilous" years of junior high.

The direction they take largely depends on the balance between the freedom, guidance, and control given by you, the parent.

It is important during this time to communicate with your child and help her understand the changes she is experiencing. Junior high brings a new academic environment, a new social awareness, and often, a changing body.

Because each child is different, it is important that you apply whatever data is in this chapter to your child and her situation.

DEALING WITH JUNIOR HIGH SCHOOLERS

Whenever someone asks me what age group I work with, my answer brings the same inevitable response. The conversation goes something like this:

"Oh, you're a teacher. What do you teach?"
"Junior high school English."
"Junior high school! Ohmygod! How come you're smiling?"

Obviously, contact with junior high school kids is not considered an enviable position. Why, then, *am* I smiling?

I'll tell you—it's because I love kids in junior high school. They're alive, growing, changing, testing their wings, a little scared, defiant, and are at a very important crossroad. They are on the brink of a major discovery; they are about to find out who they are. How difficult and successful their discovery will be is largely up to the adults around them, especially you—the parent.

If you have a child who is junior high school age, you are faced with two major problems: (1) How do you help your child grow and expand without giving her so much freedom that she gets out of control? (2) How do you give your child enough guidance and control without suppressing her into a submissive wimp?

ESTABLISH GOOD COMMUNICATION

The most basic of all solutions is good communication. If you and your child have good communication, many of the problems you encounter during the junior high years (or at any point in your child's life) can be minimized, even eliminated.

In this section we present some basic guidelines to help you establish good communication.

Create an Atmosphere in Which Your Child Will Feel Free to Communicate

Your child has to believe that when she speaks, you will believe what she says is important and will *listen with genuine interest*. As much as possible, avoid attacking your child, putting her down, making her wrong for what she is saying. Realize that your child *does* have a viewpoint and even though you may disagree with it, your communication with her will be better if you listen to and try to understand her viewpoint.

Communicate Your Viewpoints to Your Child

Often parents go to one of two extremes in communicating with their children. At one extreme, the parents allow the child total freedom of expression. What can happen in this case is that the child "takes over"—expressing her ideas and opinions without getting any parental or adult viewpoint. At the other extreme, the parents impose their viewpoint on the child without allowing the child to speak up. In this case, the child may suffer silently and decide that her viewpoint is worthless, or she may become openly defiant and rebellious. Either way, the parents have a problem if they don't recognize the need for a give and take—a true balance in communication.

Good communication involves a two-way flow. Let your child know you and hear your points of view. But try not to overwhelm her by being overbearing about your viewpoints. Work to maintain an exchange with your child. Listen to her. You will often find you have more in agreement than you may have thought. This will be especially true when your child has problems similar to those you may have had when you were her age. Tell her about what happened to *you*. The way you handled your problem may not be appropriate to your child's situation, but it will give her a different viewpoint to look at, and a feeling that her parents understand and empathize—and this can't help but bring you closer.

Take Your Child's Ideas Seriously

One of my students once asked me, "How come you never send us to the office?"

My answer, "Well, I just don't seem to have many discipline problems."

"How come?"

The answer to that took some thought. It basically comes down to the fact that whenever one of my students has an upset, I take the time to talk with her. And I remember! I remember being young, having problems, feeling that my upset was all-important. When I remember this, the child's problem becomes very understandable to me. I listen. I understand how the child feels.

Just letting the child know I understand helps. The child is willing to communicate more with me and is also willing to listen to me because my understanding makes me more real to her.

Recalling how you have felt in school and in situations similar to ones your child may be facing will help you to understand your child better and take her more seriously.

Allow Time to Talk with Your Child

Make sure you allow time in your day for talking with your child. This should be your time with your child and the communication between the two of you should take priority over all other things. (This does not mean that you have to maintain a regimented time during which you *must* talk with her. Don't force communication if none is needed.) During this time you can discuss problems your child may be having and what things are going well. The topics can vary, but try to gear it at some point to her schooling.

In the "Things to Do" section there is a survey for you to use to evaluate how well you communicate with your child. Work at improving those points until you feel confident that your communication with your child is open, growing, and meaningful.

THE PRESSURE OF PEER GROUPS

As a child grows she becomes more aware, and her world expands with this growing awareness. First she is very self-centered. Later, she becomes aware of others—those in her family. And she comes to see that sometimes others' needs and wants come into conflict with her own. However, the child also learns that this family can support her; it is something she is part of.

During the junior high school years the child becomes a young adult; awareness now extends more than ever to groups outside the family. With this new dimension a person comes to a new realization; if she wishes to "belong" to a group, she must go along with the demands and values of that group. This is often expressed to parents by such statements as:

"All the kids are going."
"Joanne and Donna wear shorts to school, so why can't I?"
"I'm the only one without a minibike."

Remember the groups formed in your junior high school days?—the smart kids, the bad kids (they smoked, said "bad" words, cut classes), the athletes (the cheerleaders and varsity stars), the artistic kids, and so on.

When your child goes to junior high school there is a very different atmosphere than is usually found in elementary school. Classes are departmentalized. This means your child will have one teacher for English, another for math, yet another for science, and so on. In most cases your child will not have the same group of classmates in each class. This situation often leads to the formation of various social groups which become a sort of defense against anonymity and a feeling of not belonging.

Even if your child does not belong to a particular group, she probably has several friends who stay together, do things together, and share their thoughts and feelings with one another. This group tends to form its own values and ideals.

Group Pressure Versus Family Values—
How to Minimize the Problem

Often a conflict can arise between the values or needs of the group your child belongs to and the values and needs of the family. For instance,

> Your daughter comes in wearing enough makeup on her eyes each day to cover the L.A. Rams backfield in a fine layer of black smudge.
>
> Your son decides homework is for twerps.
>
> You hear a conversation among your daughter's friends. They feel shoplifting is okay as long as they don't get caught.

To overcome these differences in values between the group and the family, and the conflict such differences are likely to create for your child, it is important to establish the basic values for your child early in life. If she has made these values her own, she will weigh them carefully against the values of the group.

If you find your child is picking up attitudes and values that are opposed to the ones you have tried to instill, establish where she developed them, and what her reasoning is for the changes.

Stay in communication with your child to assure her of your support. Remember, the group can exert tremendous pressure at times, and it is necessary for your child to feel there is someone who will help her maintain her own viewpoint.

It is also important to be aware that, because the junior high years involve growth and experimentation, there are some things your child will do just because everyone else is doing them. Be certain you judge whether or not your child's new behavior, attitudes, and values are harmful to her, or simply something that needs going through. Only your good sense and judgment will be able to answer that difficult question.

Here's an example:

As a teenager on my way to womanhood, I lived with my older sister and her family. I remember coming home from a babysitting job when I was about sixteen. While babysitting I had been experimenting with makeup and when I arrived home, my eyes looked as if I had slammed them into adjacent doorknobs. My sister howled with laughter, but my aunt, who was visiting, ranted and raved that I was becoming a tramp, was being poorly raised, was on the road to ruin, and so on.

My aunt's attitude showed that she could not differentiate between an important value and a fad. My sister on the other hand, was aware that teenagers are "funny" people who will eat goldfish or suffocate in phone booths, just because that's what's being done. I was a good student, a helpful child, earned my own money; my sister knew a little black pencil on my eyes couldn't ruin me.

Your Child's Individuality Versus Peer Pressure— Helping Your Child Establish Her Own Viewpoint

Another possible problem your child can encounter during junior high school is that of a conflict arising between her individuality and the demands of the group. This can often be very painful.

You can be helpful to your child by helping her to establish and maintain her own individual viewpoint. Help your child decide what she feels is important in life. Help her to know her goals, values, and purposes (see sections on decision making in Chapters Seven and Ten). Do not insist or even expect these choices to become a carbon copy of your own. Support your child in her decisions.

One thing is very important. There is a fine line between what you believe is harmful and what you just disagree with. Be as objective as possible in helping your child come to decisions. If your child makes a decision you cannot possibly condone, and she insists upon going ahead with her plans despite all objections from you, at least do this much; let your child know the door to communication is *always* open.

To help your child focus on her values and attitudes, it might be helpful to use the following list as a direction for discussion. You can and should add questions (or eliminate questions) according to what is relevant to your situation.

1. What are the things you most value in a friend?
2. What do you think are the things most worth having in life?
3. What do you value most about school? Least about school?
4. Are there any things your friends do or believe in that you disagree with? What are they? Do you feel secure enough to voice your disagreement?
5. What things about yourself do you feel are worthwhile? What would you like to change?
6. What are the things you really respect in a person? Which of your friends really have these qualities?
7. Do you feel that a person should maintain her or his individuality? Should a person go along with the group even if she or he disagrees?
8. Think of some things you'd like to have in life. What do you feel you'll have to do to get them? What would you have to be to do this?
9. Do you think school is important? How so?

PUBERTY AND SEX—
MYSTERY, WONDER, AND WORRY

There is a great deal of mystery about sex in the Western culture. This might seem a bit strange; if we're bombarded by talk, pictures, and songs about sex, how can it be a mystery?

The answer to that is fairly simple. Until a person truly knows for herself through observation and experience what something is, that thing is to some degree a mystery. The more she hears about that thing without experiencing it for herself, the more she wants to know about it. Sometimes a person hears fantastic things about an experience someone has had, so she tries it for herself and very often it doesn't seem like what that other person described. She figures she really hasn't got it yet, and may try again. This description can fit anything from sex to skiing to drugs. A person could also get very anxious about this thing and think, "What's wrong with me? I didn't feel the way everyone says I should!"

In junior high your child's body is changing. That body is now able to function in ways which our society says aren't okay yet. It's like owning a car but not knowing how to drive. Everyone tells you how marvelous it is, but no one will teach you how to drive "until you can handle it." So you sneak out and take the car for a drive. Maybe you crash, or maybe you have a great time. In any case, it wasn't okay to drive the car, but only because you weren't totally ready for the responsibility.

Teach Your Children About Sex

First of all, your child must be taught about sex so that by the time she gets to junior high she knows enough about it so that it doesn't involve the kind of mystery she feels she must immediately explore. If sex is something you find difficult to talk about, get into the topic gradually and make use of the many books on sex education that are available for all age groups, or have someone you trust (and with whom your child feels comfortable) discuss the topic. Find out what questions your child has; find out if there's anything in sex that is frightening to her.

Discuss with your child what responsibilities go hand in hand with sex. The emotional well-being of the other person involved and the possibility of bearing children should be brought up. If your child realizes that she is not ready to handle bringing up a child, the next question is, should she then try it out at the possible expense of others?

Help Your Child See Her Responsibility Regarding Sex

One of my students came into my class wearing a T-shirt that said, "If it feels good, do it." Other T-shirts at the school were even more suggestive, and some didn't even suggest—they stated openly: for example, "I'm A Virgin. This is a very old T-shirt."

I asked my student, "What kind of reaction could you expect from a shirt like that?" She became a bit flustered and said, "I don't know."

The point is that children of junior high school age should be taught to judge what kind of sexual impact their behavior and clothes might have on others. They need to be aware of what kind of effect they create by the things they say and do and even wear. This goes for both boys and girls.

If your child—boy or girl—finds he or she is getting lots of the wrong kind of attention in school, discuss what it is that is attracting that type of attention. Parents must help their children see that it is up to the individual to behave in a way that will elicit respect from others. Many children of this age "follow the crowd" and may not be aware of the suggestiveness or implied invitation in their actions—but you can help them learn to think about such things and be more responsible.

Growing Pains

In my second year of teaching I encountered a little girl in the hall who seemed to be on the verge of tears. I brought her to my room and tried to find out what was disturbing her. She told me that some boys has been bothering her. At first this was a little hard to believe because I took it in the wrong context. Before my eyes was a skinny child of 12, and yet the boys were "bothering" her. "They make fun of me. They call me skinny and say I don't wear a bra!" she said, as she burst into tears.

I really understood how she felt. She would probably have been surprised to find out that earlier in the week one of my students had been filled with grief over the fact that all the boys teased her for being "so big on the top."

These girls were both suffering from "growing pains," or lack of them (and so, probably, were the teasing boys). Strangely enough, if the too-slender girl had been in sixth grade in elementary school, rather than in the sixth grade of JHS, then she might not have been teased, and furthermore would probably not have been upset about her lack of womanly shape. If the other young lady, who was in the ninth grade, had been in high school, she probably would have no problems either.

But junior high school is a very different environment than elementary school. It isolates its members and magnifies the situations they are in. It's not just that certain children are rapidly growing and changing—*all* the students are growing, and so awareness about this area is heightened.

It's essential that children learn *before* junior high to be comfortable with their bodies and the changes that will take place. When children have a lot of worries and concerns about their bodies, point out to them that people of that age have bodies that grow and change to prepare for adulthood. Try to explain specifically the reasons for each of these changes. If you don't feel able to handle this topic, have someone in your family, a close friend, or a trusted family doctor talk to your child. There are also many books that deal with the topic (see the end of the chapter).

Most of all, help your child realize that being a *person* is more important than being a body.

Survey

	yes	sometimes	no
Does your child come to you freely to discuss matters that concern her?			
Do you feel comfortable talking with your child about any subject?			
Do you make time to talk with your child?			
Do you take a real interest in what your child has to say?			
Do you grant that what your child is saying and feeling is important?			
Can you remember your own childhood years and relate your experiences to your child's viewpoints?			
Do you allow your child the freedom *not* to communicate (especially during a time of particular anger or upset, when it might be best to let her cool down or become less upset before talking with her)?			
Do you allow your child to maintain her privacy by not insisting on knowing everything she does?			
Do you avoid constantly lecturing, as opposed to discussing things, with your child?			
Do you avoid putting down or in other ways minimizing what your child is feeling and communicating?			

THINGS TO DO

◆ *Evaluate your communication with your child.* Complete the following survey, then have your child complete it. Be objective and honest in evaluating yourself based on both your own and your child's responses to the survey questions. Then decide on what things you should continue doing, what things you should start doing, and what things you should stop doing.

Make those decisions based on the final results you want to have with your child, as far as communication is concerned. It might be helpful to write out your personal policy for establishing the kind of communication you want with your child.

◆ *Discuss with your child the responses to the survey.* Together, agree on what will be continued, started, or stopped. You can write up your policy (rules and guidelines) for communication with each other. Then decide on what things are most important to change, and concentrate on improving those things first.

◆ *Find different and fun ways to communicate.* For example, if you have difficulty communicating verbally about a certain topic, write notes to each other exchanging viewpoints, or make tape-recorded messages. Or you can arrange to give each other a set amount of time to speak frankly while the other person must *only* listen. Create a private code that only you and your child know.

Activities like these can greatly enhance your ability to

communicate with each other, especially if you and/or your child are having difficulty communicating.

◆ ***Remember how you felt when you were in junior high school.***   Getting more in touch with yourself and your past experiences can help you get closer to your child, because you can better understand and appreciate the problems and situations she is facing or may face.

For example, can you remember such things as your changing body? Wanting to know about and experience sex? Dating? How was your communication with your parents? What was good? What would you have liked to change? What groups did you belong to, or want to be part of? What kooky, rebellious, defiant, fun, or fad things did you do that perhaps your parents frowned upon? Can you remember some special uplifting moments with your parents? What was important to you that your parents understood? Didn't understand?

◆ ***Provide your child with a sound sex education.***   Give or help your child find information appropriate to her level of understanding. Be truthful in answering her questions. Express your values and beliefs about sex and experiencing sex. Let your child know where you stand about her having sexual relations.

If you have difficulty communicating about sex (or any topic), first talk about some area in that subject about which you feel comfortable. Then approach the more difficult areas, one at a time, telling your child about your discomfort. She may feel the same discomfort, and being honest about that can help both of you. Birth control information is something you should be prepared to provide. In the section below are helpful sources of information about birth control and other topics related to sex education.

SOME HELPFUL READING

Information on Sex Education

The American Association of Sex Educators and Counselors,
5010 Wisconsin Avenue, N.W.
Washington, D.C. 20016

Sex Information and Education Council of the United States (SIECUS),
1855 Broadway,
New York, N.Y. 10023

Books for Adolescents

FACTS ABOUT SEX—A BASIC GUIDE, by *Sol Gordon,* illustrated by Vivien Cohen (New York: The John Day Co., 1970).

LOVE AND SEX IN PLAIN LANGUAGE, by *Eric W. Johnson* (New York: Lippincott, 1970).

BOYS AND SEX, by *Wardell B. Pomeroy* (New York: Delacorte Press, 1968).

Books for Parents

YOUR CHILD AND SEX—A GUIDE FOR PARENTS, by *Wardell B. Pomeroy* (New York: Delacorte Press, 1974).

chapter 14

Some Final Thoughts

In this closing chapter I would like to present some viewpoints and information on several topics that may prove helpful in ensuring that your child's years in school will be valuable and successful.

IF YOUR CHILD HAS A PROBLEM IN SCHOOL

As your child goes through school, some of the more typical problems he may encounter are boredom, not getting along with his teacher, difficulty with specific subjects, underachievement, problems with other children, not liking or wanting to go to school. When these or other problems arise, you should do your best to devise a basic approach that will help you find out the real reason(s) for the problem. Only then can you take appropriate steps to handle the situation.

I suggest that you establish a procedure to organize your way of handling school problems. For example:

1. Decide what the ideal situation should be in relation to the problem area.

2. Determine the real facts by observation, discussion, and questioning of any appropriate individuals.
3. Locate the most important reason(s) why things are *not* as they should ideally be.
4. Work out a way to handle the reason(s), beginning with what you consider the most important one.
5. Work always toward achieving the ideal situation.

Here's an example of a problem I handled using the above format.

The *problem* concerned Nathanial, a fourth-grade student who was often truant and had a very negative attitude toward school.

The *ideal situation* was for Nathanial to want to be in school so much that he would come early and stay late.

The *facts* were that Nathanial had been previously held back a grade, read two years below grade level, had parents who rarely responded to requests for conferences, would not discuss his problems and upsets with me, did not complete any of his classwork or homework, and was constantly in trouble for disruptive behavior.

The *most important reason* why he did not want to be in school was that his backlog of failure, frustration, and difficulty caused him to have no real purpose or interest in what school had to offer him.

The *way to handle the problem* was to use his abilities and strengths in some way that would give him successes and create a purpose that would make him want to be in school.

I made a point to get in touch with Nathanial's mother to learn more about what he enjoyed and did well at outside of school. I also spoke with a couple of his former teachers for the same reason. I found out that Nathanial was very handy, and loved to fix and create things with his hands.

It wasn't long after my talk with Nathanial's mother when something happened that led to a dramatic change in his attitude toward school. Hammy, the class hamster, disappeared from his tank. "Aha!" I thought to myself, "a perfect setup to handle Nathanial."

The class was upset about losing Hammy. Then we began to hear him scratching around behind the radiator. We made many unsuccessful attempts that day to capture him. At 3 o'clock, as the class was leaving I pulled Nathanial aside and said, "I need your help to build a trap to catch Hammy."

"Yeah, sure," he answered, trying to seem indifferent. But his eyes sparkled as he fought to keep from smiling and showing his obvious enthusiasm and surprise at my request for help.

Nathanial designed and built a simple, yet ingeniously effective trap that I never could have thought of. I was very impressed (and so was Nathanial).

The next morning I arrived at school an hour early as I always did, and there was the usually half-hour-late Nathanial waiting for me in front of the school. We quickly went up to our room and quietly opened the door. I had my fingers, eyes, legs, toes, and arms crossed hoping Hammy had been caught in Nathanial's trap. And sure enough— there was Hammy, sound asleep—caught!

To see that smile of pride and satisfaction cross Nathanial's face was a joyous moment for me. From that day on he changed. His ability and fame spread throughout the school— I made sure of that. He was frequently called upon to help solve and handle various fix-it problems around the class and school.

Needless to say, Nathanial lost his negative attitude toward school. Furthermore, he often showed up early and left late. That problem was solved.

DIFFERENTIATE BETWEEN FACT AND OPINION

I've touched on this topic in a few other places in the book, but I feel it's important enough to require further discussion.

A *fact* is something that can be proven by actual evidence; it's a provable truth.

An *opinion* is an evaluation, judgment, or statement that may or may not have a basis in fact; it's a personal feeling or sentiment.

To mistake your child's, his teacher's, or anyone's statement of opinion as fact can cause many unnecessary problems. Such statements as "My teacher hates me and always picks on me," or "Your child has no self-control and is very rude," if taken at face value can portray your child or his teacher in a very bad light and may cause you to take actions that really were unnecessary when the actual facts were found out.

If a school puts a *label* on your child (hyperactive, mentally retarded, gifted, and so on), find out whether this label represents opinion or fact. A label can greatly affect (both negatively and positively, depending on the label) the way a child is perceived by others and by himself. It's all too easy to assume that a label is correct. What if your child were labeled "mentally retarded" because of his inability to do well academically, and he was then placed in a program developed for mentally retarded students. And suppose it was later found that he'd had an undetected hearing problem that caused him to *appear* mentally retarded. Wouldn't you be disturbed that you had not questioned the label in the first place?

Your responsibility is to find out the facts that are the

basis of any opinions formed by your child, his teacher, or any other relevant person.

LEARNING DISABILITY AND HYPERACTIVITY

In a small percentage of cases a child may have trouble learning because of a learning disability (a problem apparently unrelated to mental retardation, any physical handicap—including vision and hearing—emotional difficulties, environmental neglect, and hardships). With a learning disability a child can have normal or above-average intelligence, but may have trouble perceiving and/or expressing himself verbally or in writing. He may have trouble distinguishing between similar words and letters: (*stay* and *stop, b* and *d*). He may write mirror fashion (*p* becomes *q*).

Be very cautious about having the label "learning-disabled" applied to your child. Far too often teachers and other school personnel apply this label because they can't deal with the learning problems of a child due to their own inability, lack of experience, and knowledge; lack of patience; or a failure to recognize that a child's learning problems may be caused by "normal" developmental or learning patterns—for example, it's a common mistake for children first learning how to read to confuse words that are similar.

"Hyperactivity" is another label that is frequently used carelessly. This label may be used for a child who is a behavior problem because he can't sit still, is easily distracted and disturbed, and tends to act impulsively. I've had children placed in my class, who some labeled as hyperactive. They did beautifully with proper handling—that is, when I consistently "enforced" exactly what their freedoms and limits were and got them interested and involved in class work and activities.

Don't accept any label placed on your child without making sure a complete battery of tests is done, including an intelligence test, a physical checkup, an evaluation of your child's emotional health, an evaluation of his ability to perceive and express verbal and written language. Your child may have a true learning disability or be hyperactive and need special instruction and handling. I would only agree to those labels being placed on a child if all other possibilities for that child's apparent inability to learn and behave have been carefully checked out—especially such things as whether correct study methods and skills are being used, proper work habits are being applied, the physical well being of the child has been checked.

A booklet that discusses the topics of hyperactive and learning-disabled children in an informative way is *How to*

Handle the Hyperactive Child. You can get copies of this booklet and further information by writing to The Committee for the Protection of Patients' Rights, P.O. Box 10314, Clearwater, Florida 33517.

IF YOUR CHILD IS BORED

Children are too often bored with school; this is especially true for gifted children. There are several common reasons for boredom. The child may see no relevance or purpose for what he's studying. He may have no interest in the material he's studying—the work may simply not be challenging enough. The methods and teaching style of the teacher may be inappropriate for the student (for example, he may need a more flexible classroom structure in which he can more easily pursue his own ideas and interests).

What you as a parent can do if your child is bored in school depends largely on what is causing the boredom. Find out and discuss with your child and his teacher ways to provide challenging, motivating experiences and activities. Perhaps a special program could be worked out for your child in his class, or in the school.

You might want to check out the possibility of sending your child to another school—one that may have a better learning environment for him. There are schools that specialize in certain curriculum areas, such as music and art, science, or various vocational subjects. Different schools provide different educational programs—some have more flexible scheduling and methods of teaching, others offer a more strict and rigid type of scheduling and programming.

Discuss the alternatives that are best for your child with the school guidance counselor, teacher, or one of the supervisors.

BEHAVIOR PROBLEMS

The causes for school behavior problems are varied. Among the more common reasons are that the child fails to apply, because of his own or his teacher's neglect, good methods of study, causing a lack of success at learning which leads to frustration, upset, and ultimately poor behavior. Also, some teachers can't control a group of children. Some children have no real interest in the material being studied, so they become bored and restless, and poor behavior results. Or a child may have physical problems, especially those connected with nutrition. Still another cause of behavior problems is peer-group influence—a child may go along with his friends' misbehavior or something outside school may have upset the child, causing him to behave badly. Or perhaps he has had a personal conflict with another student or the teacher.

The way you handle your child's behavior problem depends on the specific cause(s). No matter how you approach the problem, be sure the child has a meaningful purpose, and that he achieves success and has his success acknowledged by others. Also, every child should be allowed to contribute to the class in some way. Make sure that your child knows what his limits and freedoms are. Help him develop the basics of good study, to make sure he will indeed learn. Handle any upsets your child may have outside of school, so these don't impinge on the school situation.

FOR THE HIGH SCHOOLER'S PARENTS*

The high school years are marked by changes, frustrations, new experiences, and physical and emotional growth. There are several ways you can help your child get through these years happily and well prepared for the adult years.

Don't Change Your Basic Values and Style
Because of the Changes Your Child is Going Through

Children of high school (and junior high school) are deeply involved in trying to find their way, their identity in life. They may experiment and "try on" various behaviors, attitudes, values, and lifestyles. What they want is to see examples of different viewpoints, try some of these out, and come to their own decision about who they are.

When your child knows he can depend on you to maintain your basic viewpoints and parental style, it helps provide a base of certainty upon which he can rely as he ventures out into an uncertain world. Maintain your position, be certain and consistent in your beliefs and style, and don't be afraid to take a stand when you believe it's needed and wanted.

Recognize that your child will go through changes in behavior, attitudes, and values. Try not to see each change as being the final outcome of your child's experimentation process. Your daughter probably won't always wear purple fingernail polish; your son is more than likely to put on a three-piece suit *sometime* in the future.

---

* This section is based on conversations I have had with Sheila Mackenzie, a former high school teacher who is currently working with and counseling parents and their high school children.

Be Sure Your Child Has Enough to Do

It's when your child is bored and restless that problems all too easily develop. Help him find jobs, give him added responsibilities. As we stressed in earlier chapters, keep your child meaningfully busy. As your child starts the tenth grade, ask him to think about what he would like to have, do, and be in the next few years. This will help provide meaningful purpose and direction to his life.

Show Your Child You Care

When children enter high school, this doesn't mean you automatically slack off in your concern. At this point your child especially needs you to care, help, participate, and take responsibility in his schooling. Show up for parent-teacher conferences; observe your child's classes when possible; go to ball games, school shows, or any activities in which your child is participating. Staying actively involved and participating in your child's schooling is a good way to maintain or help establish good communication with him.

Be Ready to Help Your Child Out of Trouble

Chances are that as your child is spreading his wings and trying different patterns of flight he will run into some trouble. Be there for him! Be honest, truthful, and willing to sweat and work hard to help your child sort out and handle all obstacles and problems. If your child gets into trouble of some sort, understand that he really wants help and hang in there.

Show Your Love

In too many parent-child relationships, there is an apparent belief that as a child grows older, and especially as he reaches the teen years, there is less need for parents to openly show and express love, interest, and admiration for their children. This is absolutely untrue. When was the last time you hugged or kissed your child, or told him that you really care for and love him? Try it—it will make you both feel good. It's the basic ingredient, throughout a long process of education, in helping your child in school. And its effects will last a lifetime, for both of you.

Bibliography

Adler, Mortimer J. and *Charles Van Doren.* How to Read a Book. New York: Simon and Schuster, 1972.

Armstrong, William H. Study Tips—How to Effectively Get Better Grades. Woodbury, New York: Barron's Educational Series, Inc., 1975.

Becker, George J. Television and the Classroom Reading Program. Newark, Delaware: International Reading Association, 1973.

Bell, Terrel H. Active Parent Concern. Englewood Cliffs, New Jersey: Prentice-Hall, Inc., 1976.

Bell, Terrel H. "What Makes a Good Teacher," American Educator, 1, no.1 (Winter 1977).

Brecher, Edward M., and the Editors of Consumer Reports. The Consumers Union Report, Licit and Illicit Drugs. Boston, Toronto: Little, Brown & Company, 1972.

Brown, Doris and *Pauline McDonald.* Learning Begins at Home. Los Angeles: Lawrence Publishing Co., 1969.

Chall, Jeanne. Reading 1967–1977, A Decade of Change and Promise. Bloomington, Indiana: The Phi Delta Kappan Foundation, 1977.

Chess, Stella, M.D., with *Jane Whitbread.* How to Help Your Child Get the Most Out of School. Garden City, New York: Doubleday & Co., Inc., 1974.

Cohen, Sidney, M.D. The Drug Dilemma. New York: McGraw-Hill Book Company, 1969.

Cole, Luella. Students Guide to Efficient Study. New York: Holt, Rinehart and Winston, 1960.

Collins, Myrtle T., and *Dwane R. Collins.* Survival Kit for Teachers (and Parents). Pacific Palisades, California: Goodyear Publishing Co., Inc., 1975.

The Committee for the Protection of Patients' Rights. How to Handle the Hyperactive Child. Clearwater, Florida, 1978.

Cook, C.C. and *A.O. Thomas,* eds. Basic Study Manual—Compiled from the Works of L. Ron Hubbard. Los Angeles: Applied Scholastics, Inc., 1972.

Corbin, Charles B., Ph. D. Becoming Physically Educated in the Elementary School (2nd edition). Philadelphia: Lea & Febiger, 1976.

Daly, Margaret. "Schools: What Are Your Legal Rights," Better Homes & Gardens, 56, no.4 (April 1978).

Daly, Margaret. "You and Your School Board: How to Make Your Ideas Count," Better Homes & Gardens, 55,no.12 (December 1977).

Doman, Glenn J. How to Teach Your Baby to Read. New York: Random House, Inc., 1963.

Dunn, Rita, Kenneth Dunn, and *Gary E. Price.* "Diagnosing Learning Styles: a Prescription for Avoiding Malpractice Suits," Phi Delta Kappan, 58, no.5 (January 1977).

Divoky, Diane. "How to Grade a Teacher," Parents Magazine, 3, no. 9 (September 1978).

Fair, Virginia. "Spotlight Professional of the Month—Glenn Doman," TODAY'S PROFESSIONALS, Issue III, 1978.

Flesch, Rudolph, Paul Witty, et al. HOW YOU CAN BE A BETTER STUDENT. New York: Sterling Publishing Co., Inc., 1957.

Frank, Peter R., "Drug Abuse Is Alive and Well," EDUCATIONAL FORUM, 42, no.4 (May 1978).

Gillham, Peter F. FUNDAMENTALS OF SUCCESS, Red Baron Publishing Co., 1972.

Goodacre, Elizabeth. SCHOOL AND HOME. London: National Foundation for Educational Research in England and Wales, 1970.

Gurney, David W. "Judging Effective Teaching," PHI DELTA KAPPAN, 58, no. 10 (June 1977).

Haefele, Donald L. "The Teacher Perceiver Interview: How Valid?" PHI DELTA KAPPAN, 59, no. 10 (June 1978).

"How to Help Your Kids in School," BETTER HOMES & GARDENS, 55, no. 11 (November 1977).

Hubbard, L. Ron. CHILD DIANETICS. Los Angeles, California: The Church of Scientology of California, 1968.

——— THE PROBLEMS OF WORK. Los Angeles: The Church of Scientology of California, 1972.

——— SCIENTOLOGY: NEW SLANT ON LIFE. Los Angeles: The Church of Scientology of California, 1968.

——— SCIENTOLOGY: THE FUNDAMENTALS OF THOUGHT. Los Angeles: The Church of Scientology of California, 1973.

Hymes, James L., Jr. EFFECTIVE HOME-SCHOOL RELATIONS. Sierra Madre, California: The Southern California Association for the Education of Young Children, 1974.

Kaye, Evelyn. THE FAMILY GUIDE TO CHILDREN'S TELEVISION. New York: Pantheon Books, 1974.

Knows, R.M. "What Me Study? Some Suggestions to Make a Hard Job Easier," AMERICAN BIOLOGY TEACHER, 39 (March 1977).

Lieberman, Florence, Phyllis Caroff, and *Mary Gottesfeld.* BEFORE ADDICTION—HOW TO HELP YOUTH. New York: Behavioral Publications, 1973.

Liebert, Robert M., John M. Neale, and *Emily S. Davidson.* THE EARLY WINDOW—EFFECTS OF TELEVISION ON CHILDREN AND YOUTH. New York: Pergamon Press, Inc., 1973.

Lockhart, Aileene S. and *Howard S. Slusher.* CONTEMPORARY READINGS IN PHYSICAL EDUCATION (3rd edition). Dubuque, Iowa: Wm. C. Brown Company, Publishers, 1975.

McVey, G.F. "Modifying the Home into a Learning Environment," EDUCATION, 91, no. 11 (April–May 1971).

Mankiewicz, Frank and *Joel Swerdlow.* REMOTE CONTROL. New York: Quadrangle, 1977.

Melton, David. HOW TO HELP YOUR PRESCHOOLER LEARN ... MORE ... FASTER ... AND BETTER. New York: David McKay Co., Inc., 1976.

Miller, Mary Susan and *Samm Sinclair Baker.* STRAIGHT TALK TO PARENTS. New York: Stein & Day Publishers, 1976.

Minshull, Ruth. MIRACLES FOR BREAKFAST. Ann Arbor: Scientology, 1968.

Morgan, Clifford T. and *James Reese.* HOW TO STUDY. New York, Toronto, London: McGraw-Hill Book Company, Inc., 1957.

Morris, Norman S. TELEVISION'S CHILD. Boston, Toronto: Little, Brown & Company, 1971.

Nason, Leslie J., Ed.D. HELP YOUR CHILD SUCCEED IN SCHOOL. New York: The Associated Press Cornerstone Library Publications, 1964.

Percy, Bernard, ed. How to Grow a Child ... A Child's Advice to Parents. Los Angeles: Price/Stern/Sloan Publishers, Inc., 1978.

Rabbit, James A. "The Parent/Teacher Conference: Trauma or Teamwork," Phi Delta Kappan, 59, no.7 (March 1978).

Reading Laboratory, Inc. Study Faster and Retain More. Cleveland: The World Publishing Co., 1964.

Reisman, F. "Students Learning Styles: How to Determine, Strengthen and Capitalize on Them," Today's Education, 65, (S' 1976).

Rogers, Vincent and *Joan Baron.* "Teaching Styles and Pupil Progress," Phi Delta Kappan, 58, no.8 (April 1977).

Schimmel, David and *Louis Fischer.* The Rights of Parents in the Education of Their Children. Columbia, Maryland: The National Committee for Citizens in Education, 1977.

Shaw, Harry, 30 Ways to Improve Your Grades. New York: McGraw-Hill Book Company, 1976.

Smith, Cam, What it is, What it Ain't. Published by Cam Smith, 1972.

Stevens, Andrew, Techniques for Handling Problem Parents. Englewood Cliffs, New Jersey: Prentice-Hall, Inc., 1966.

Thweatt, W.H. "Vicious Circle in Study Problems," Personnel and Guidance Journal, 54 (May 1976).

Tussing, Lyle. Study and Succeed. New York: John Wiley & Sons, Inc., 1962.

Uslander, Arlene and *Caroline Weiss,* with the editors of Learning Magazine. Dealing with Questions about Sex. Palo Alto, California: Learning Handbooks, 1975.

Walter, Tim and *Al Siebert*. STUDENT SUCCESS—HOW TO BE A BETTER STUDENT AND STILL HAVE TIME FOR YOUR FRIENDS. New York: Holt, Rinehart and Winston, 1960.

Winn, Marie. THE PLUG-IN DRUG. New York: The Viking Press, 1974.

Yelon, Stephen and *Grace W. Weinstein.* A TEACHER'S WORLD, PSYCHOLOGY IN THE CLASSROOM. New York: McGraw-Hill, Inc., 1977.

Index

Academics, 98–99
Accomplishment, expectations of, 74, 77
Acknowledgment of skills, 73, 77
Action, 47, 60–62, 68, 75, 77
Action For Children's Television (ACT), 193–94
Activity, meaningful, 5–6, 18, 120–21, 223
Addiction (see Drugs and Alcohol abuse)
Addiction Research Foundation of Ontario, 129
Additives, food, 131, 133, 136
Adrenalin, 134
Aerosols, 118, 129
Agreements, 4–5, 13–15, 17, 192
Airplane glue, 118
Alcohol (see Drugs and alcohol abuse)
Alexander Graham Bell Association for the Deaf, 160
Almanacs, 70
American Association of Sex Educators and Counselors, 212
American Optometric Association (AOA), 147–52, 160, 191–92, 194
Amphetamines, 116, 129
Angel dust (PCP), 117, 129
Application and understanding, 70–72, 76, 78

Approval, 6, 17, 18, 72
Arthur, Ann, 121
Assignments, completion of, 3, 5–8, 10–14
Astigmatism, 149
Atlas, 70
Atmosphere, 21–22
Audiovisual aids, 86
Axioms and Logics (Hubbard), 60

Barbiturates, 116, 129
Basic Study Manual (Hubbard), 60, 76n
Basic study principles, 41, 47, 60–67, 68, 75, 98
Be, concept of, 16
Behavior problems, 221
Benzedrine, 116
Birth control, 211
Blood-sugar levels, 134–35
Boredom, 6, 61–62, 220–21, 223
Bulletin boards, 83–85

Cannabis, 112, 117
Carbohydrates, 135, 137
Career education, 161–71
  basic viewpoint, 162–64
  guidance, 164–67
  programs, 168–70
Charts, 14, 17–19, 77, 85, 86

233

progress checks, 16, 17
recognizing potential, 6, 18
setting an example, 8–10, 18
starting and completing, 3, 5–8, 10–14
time schedules, 11–13

Work space, 83
Work-study policies, 13
Wright, Reggie, 122
Writing, 43, 188–89

Zerovnik, Greg, 120